Religion and Popular Culture

A Hyper-Real Testament

P.I.E. Peter Lang

Bruxelles · Bern · Berlin · Frankfurt am Main · New York · Oxford · Wien

Adam POSSAMAI

Religion and Popular Culture

A Hyper-Real Testament

"Gods, Humans and Religions"
No.7

The research, writing, and publication for this book was made possible by a grant provided from the University of Western Sydney, and also from some funds given by the Critical Social Science Research Group from the same University.

© P.I.E. PETER LANG s.a.
Éditions scientifiques universitaires
Brussels, 2005; 2nd printing 2007
1 avenue Maurice, 1050 Brussels, Belgium
info@peterlang.com; www.peterlang.com

ISSN 1377-8323
ISBN 13: 978-90-5201-272-8
US ISBN 13: 978-0-8204-6634-7
D/2005/5678/04
Printed in Germany

CIP available from the British Library, GB
and the Library of Congress, USA.

Bibliographic information published by "Die Deutsche Bibliothek"

"Die Deutsche Bibliothek" lists this publication in the "Deutsche Nationalbibliografie";
detailed bibliographic data is avalaible in the Internet at <http://dnb.ddb.de>.

Contents

Preface

For my wife, Alphia Possamai-Inesedy who has given me the strength to spend long hours on this manuscript and who was always there when I was stuck in my flow of argumentation.

I was able to finish this book thanks to a grant I received from the University of Western Sydney and to funds given by my research group, the Critical Social Sciences Research Training Concentration Group. With this money, I was able to employ two research assistants, Ashley Davis and Stephen Chavura who have provided long hours and great excitement on this project.

Also, I would like to thank my family in Belgium, my father, Angelo, my mother, Judith, and my brother, Philippe, who provided me with a mass of popular culture material when I was young. In Australia, my children Natasha and Cameron were essential in keeping me up-to-date with recent material from popular culture, and were interrogated on many occasions about the Pokemon, Harry Potter and various computer games. Thanks to my friends from Melbourne, Frank Formosa, Bernard Caleo, Arnaud Gallois and Graham St John who gave me great inspiration in my reading of popular culture. And to my colleagues from the executive committee from the Australian Association for the Study of Religions (Kath McPhillips, Merv Bendle and Carole Cusack), and from the School of Applied Social and Human Sciences at the University of Western Sydney (Mary Hawkins, Michael Bounds, Rob O'Neil and Murray Lee) who listened patiently to my discussion about *Star Wars* and vampire fictions and waited in a queue without complaining while I was overloading the staff laser printer with my long documents from the Internet. Many thanks to Simeon Payne and Phillip Johnson who opened my eyes on the world of Christianity and popular culture.

Adam Possamai

Note

Some of the chapters of this book have their origins in some articles published previously. These are:

Possamai, A. (2002) "Secrecy and Consumer Culture: An Exploration of Esotericism in Contemporary Western Society Using the Work of Simmel and Baudrillard" *Australian Religion Studies Review* 15 (1): 44-56.

Possamai, A. (2002) "Cultural Consumption of History and Popular Culture in Alternative Spiritualities" *Journal of Consumer Culture* (2) 2: 197-218.

Possamai, A. (2003) "Alternative Spiritualities and the Logic of Late Capitalism" *Culture and Religion* 4 (1): 31-45.

Possamai, A. (2003) "Alternative Spiritualities, New Religious Movements and Jediism in Australia" *Australian Religion Studies Review* 16 (2): 69-86.

Possamai, A. (forthcoming) "Superheroes and the Development of Latent Abilities: A Hyper-Real Re-enchantment?" in K. McPhillips and L. Hume (eds.) *Popular Spiritualities: The Politics of Contemporary Enchantment*, Ashgate, UK.

Introduction

In Milo Manara's graphic novel, *H.P. and Giuseppe Bergman*, Giuseppe is sent by a corporation to get out and live the Adventure. Taking his task to pleasure, and leaving his place and partner in Venice, he goes out full of excitement for the Adventure. He travels in a van through the political turmoil of the heated Italian political demonstrations of the 1960s, and then sails to South America. Under the mentoring of the Adventure expert, H.P. – who gives hardly any guidance – Giuseppe faces a range of disappointing experiences. He fails to save a woman who has been lost as a sexual object at a poker game; is captured, pants down, by Indians from the Amazon; escapes them awkwardly to be then recaptured even more awkwardly by a South American revolutionary soldier; falls gravely ill; and is decapitated "heroically" – finally – by an Indian. Until his death, Giuseppe viewed his adventure as a real failure because he was not living it the "proper heroic way". He failed in everything that he did; he did not have control of any situation; he met sumptuous women and did not have sex with them the way a hero from the period between the distribution of the pill and the discovery of AIDS would have had. Only his death gave him a feeling of accomplishment to his Adventure.

After his death, Giuseppe "psychedelically" returns to Venice and wakes up on a crowded vaporetto. He first wonders if he had a dream. But these thoughts are soon forgotten when a feeling of frustration takes place. He realises that he has not died from the glorious death that was part of his great Adventure. Frustrated by his discovery, and after he has landed in the streets of Venice, he sees his mentor, H.P. – the initials of Hugo Pratt, the Italian Maestro of graphic novels – who loses his notebook. Giuseppe finds in these pages an account of H.P.'s life in Venice. He discovers how H.P. saw this City of canals as a place of occult knowledge. In these notes, the mysterious, the mystique, the spiritual, are to be found by whoever is ready to see them in their everyday life; not necessarily by going on a long adventure in some exotic lands. The story finishes with Giuseppe and H.P. together in a governmental agency where life seems dull. Giuseppe, upset to be back in the reality of everyday life, is then asked to observe the feet of an administrative officer, who seems as exciting as an accountant going through a tax declaration. After a closer look, he realises that this boring person has two feet like a goat. The reader is left with the certitude that Adventure is everywhere for as long as one is ready to see and explore it in everyday life.

It is this type of adventure that this book hopes to offer. This hyper-real testament will open a door on an intriguing and fascinating world that is not necessarily exclusive to some exotic and/or occult groups, but that is part of our everyday life. This exoticism, that was the preserve of anthropologists exploring some far-away lands, of explorers hoping to discover unmapped territories, and of some luddite spies manipulating people to gain secret knowledge, can also be the preserve of social scientists and/or cultural observers who are ready to open their eyes to the everyday life of our postmodern world. By exploring new practices in a postmodern society, a new phenomenon that was left in the shadows of a Platonic cave since the 1960s will be brought to light; that of popular culture as a platform for religious creativity. The point of this book is the account and theorisation of a new form of spirituality that comes out of popular culture and gives meaning to many social actors. It is also the account of how certain groups such as fundamentalist groups attempt to police popular culture and prevent this religious "creativity".

However, before going on this sociological "adventure", a clarification of key interrelations between religion and art, between art and popular culture, and between popular culture and art are required to introduce the setting of this book.

Religion and Art

From a Christian perspective, the relationship between art and religion is not a simple one, especially since the gap between established religion and the arts has widened since the Renaissance. Previously, the medieval church, when not trying to ban the production of images altogether, offered the artist a controlled role as the producer of texts from the Bible for the illiterate. Art was under the patronage of the Church.

With the Romanesque style, the contemplative arts of the monasteries were sophisticated allegories and symbolism that could only be interpreted by members of the religious community. With the development of the Gothic style, religious art became directed towards the illiterate population and carried the development of Gothic cathedrals as the centre of cities and of the people's everyday life. These cathedrals were not only places of worship but could also serve as town halls and places of meeting. With late medieval styles, such as Giotto's artistic movement, the gospel became more adapted to everyday life by simplifying allegories and symbolism into simple images of life.

However, since the birth of the Renaissance, and the new role given to the artist – that of being creative – tensions started to create a distance between the controlled power of the production of images by the Church and on the independence of the artist. There was a shift away from medieval symbolism and heavenly vision towards a more accurate description of forms from the natural world. With the growth of power of nation-states, merchant and shipping families, the Church was no longer the main source of patronage.

With the advent of secularisation (see Chapter 1), the Church was also no longer the main focus of life, and artists who explored themes such as existence and the meaning of life, were doing this outside of its canvas. On the other hand, the Church also stopped viewing the artist as an ally in evangelism. Despite several attempts in the nineteenth and twentieth century such as the European Sacred Art Renewal Movement and the Blake Prize (Australia), the divorce between the Church and the artist remains strong (Crumlin, 1984).

Even if art and religion are no longer in a perfect symbiosis as in the past, there are of course works of art that can be viewed as spiritual/religious on many levels (e.g. Kandinsky, 1977; Crumlin, 1998). Pushing the argument further, Smith (1994) argues that from within some modernist movements – such as abstract and formalist art – artists were seeking to create a universal art that would express a universal religion; that is "an international style capable of expressing an international spirituality divorced from local cult rituals and ceremonies" (*o.c.*: 107).

It is worth noting that at the beginning of the twentieth century, art's iconography was mainly Judaeo-Christian. However, by the end of last century, pieces of art from, for example, Kandinsky, Tobey, Kiefer and Flack, have been influenced by other religions, such as theosophy, Eastern religions, the kabala and the Goddess movement (Crumlin, 1998: 10). Even if art can be viewed as spiritual/religious and is no longer Judaeo-Christian-centric, discussing the association between art and religion might still be a taboo, as many art critics and historians tend to affirm that art is something separate from religion. However, as Crumlin (1998) points out, religious imagination is present in all areas of life and art and religion interpenetrate.

It will be the argument of this book that religious imagination is also present in popular culture, perhaps more now than ever.

Art and Popular Culture

Popular culture – also called low culture, mass culture, and popular arts – gained an interest in the academic sphere when it stopped being opposed to art – also called high culture and fine arts – especially since the decline of modernism and the advent of postmodernism in the arts and philosophy. For the purpose of this introduction, I will understand modernism and postmodernism as a philosophy and an art movement. In the next chapter I will deal with modernity and postmodernity; that is, a change in the structure and culture of our society.

Before going further, it is important at this stage to clarify the concepts of art and popular culture as used in this book. In my clarification, I will unfortunately make some generalisations, but these are mainly for heuristic purposes. By art, I make reference to "Fine Art" such as opera, symphony, painting, sculpture, experimental performance art, ballet, literature… Art is generally displayed in museums and galleries and tends to be valorised by the upper classes. By popular culture, I include popular music (rock, pop, country, etc.), popular fiction such as graphic novels, movies (Hollywood, made-for-television and indie), television drama and sit-com, advertising (print, television)… Popular culture tends to be part of the mass media and is consumed by the masses. For the purpose of this book, I do not include folk art or extend popular culture that would include, for example, fashion, hair colouring, body design (tattoos, piercings), the beach, and manufactured products (Coca-Cola, mobile phones), sport, etc.

The term "postmodernism" became popular in the 1960s on the island of Manhattan when artists and writers such as Cage, Burroughs, Hassan and Sontag first used it. These creators were rejecting high modernism, which they viewed as "exhausted" because of its institutionalisation in the museum and in the academy. The movement gained wider usage in the 1970s and 1980s, and discussions between this movement and a new philosophy was going back and forth between the US and Europe. This lead to postmodernism as a philosophy with key theorists such as Bell, Kristeva, Lyotard, Derrida, Foucault, and Baudrillard.

The feature of postmodernism in the arts is that there can no longer be any boundary between art and everyday life; that there should no longer be a hierarchy between high and popular culture. The assumption that art is only repetition and that nothing new can be invented is also central. The movement also favours the mixing of codes, and is promiscuous in its use of artistic styles. For example, Andy Warhol led the Pop Art Movement and brought imageries of popular culture (e.g. Marilyn

Monroe, Superman, and a Campbell's can of soup) to a "high-art" canvas.

This led to the development of the study of popular culture which is now a growing field of research. Since the advent of what can be called "postmodernity" or "late modernity", everyday life and popular culture have reached the same level of recognition of high culture as a focus of study (Featherstone, 1991). Themes such as shopping, video clips, TV shows, and magazines are as well researched as Shakespeare's plays and Puccini's operas.

Today, the old border between "high" and "low" culture is not easy to recognise, as there is no longer a clear consensus within the field of cultural production and consumption. Art uses popular culture and vice versa (Walker, 1983). For example, many of today's poets are involved in rock music. Rock bands, such as Aerosmith, Metallica and Kiss perform with a philharmonic orchestra. Composers like Philip Glass synthesise classical and "popular" styles. In 2001, the Sydney Opera house marketed its operas as television shows to the larger public with the catchy blur of: "Opera: more shame than the *Weakest Link*, more tears than *All Saints*, more backstabbing than *The Mole*". As Jameson (1983: 112) explains:

> [...] many of the newer postmodernisms have been fascinated precisely by that whole landscape of advertising and motels, of the Las Vegas strip, of the late show and Grade-B Hollywood film, of so-called paraliterature with its airport paperback categories of the gothic and the romance, the popular biography, the murder mystery and the science fiction or fantasy novel. They no longer "quote" such "texts" as Joyce might have done, or a Mahler, they incorporate them, to the point where the line between high art and commercial forms seems increasingly difficult to draw.

We are no longer bound to traditional values of (dis)taste which give a general agreement on what is good and bad. In this postmodern society, there is no longer any self-evident consensus on the cultural hierarchies, such as the opposition between the high bourgeois culture and the low working class taste of the nineteenth century. The word "pluralism" has been used in some circles to describe the status of "fine arts" in the age of mass media (Walker, 1983). In this view "fine arts" are only one type of cultural activity among today's multitude of cultural sources, and are not better or worse than popular culture. Opposed to this view, some philosophy and art schools of thought continue to teach us about taste, and claim that we do not know what is high and low in this society. They refuse to accept that "fine arts" are no longer the main sources of the deepest intellectual, emotional, aesthetic, and spiritual experiences. However, cultural multiplicity has become so dominant and subcultures so many that cultures have now co-existing hierarchies that cannot be easily distinguished from one another, whether we like it or not.

It is important to note before going further that this book understands postmodernity as a cultural dominant, even a hegemonic force, in today's western world. Needless to say, not all cultural items of today are postmodern, but most of them are.

Popular Culture and Religion

This book does not understand popular culture as a sub-culture for the masses, or as a form of evasion which leads to a retreat from any socio-political activity, or as a form of control of the masses by various groups in power. Popular culture might be all of these, but it is also a medium for the autodetermination of social actors, and more specifically to this book, spiritual self-determination. Even if popular culture is part of global capitalism managed by multinational corporations, even if it provides a form of escapism from our "anxious" and/or "hidden" reality at the same level as window shopping, it is also a platform for our own biography. We live through and with it. We create our lives and view ourselves through popular culture.

Religion and popular culture co-exist intimately, and cannot be seen simply as a relationship of cause and effect. At times religion creates and regulates popular culture. Indeed, religious actors who express themselves in popular culture are also engaged in shaping popular culture, and in doing so, making possible some experiences and denying access to others. It can take the form of using the content of popular culture to back up their religion, or it can take the form of censorship towards certain narratives. At other times, popular culture can shape the form and content of religion. Some people appear to practice religion/spirituality by creatively reusing the artefacts of contemporary mass-mediated culture – e.g. images, stories, and songs from cable and broadcast television, radio, Zines – rather than following the meaning offered by religious institutions. They might view *Star Wars*, *Star Trek: The Next Generation* or *Oprah* religiously and share with other people fictional or quasi-fictional scenarios. A plethora of distinct popular faiths appear to exist alongside more mainstream religions. Popular culture can amuse, entertain, instruct, and relax people, but it is also an inspiration for religion.

The time in which we were the social reflection of our parents is gone. Their religion, ethnicity, class, political affiliation, taste and distaste are no longer so easily transmitted from one generation to another. Even if there are exceptions, the trend of today is to create one's own biography/identity. People in this postmodern age pick and choose what suits them for their identity at a specific time and place. As part of this library of choices, popular culture is on the shelf with class, religion, sexuality, significant others... (see Chapter 3). In this process, popular culture, among many other socio-cultural factors, influences the construction of the self; including that of the religious self.

As will be explored, the trend today in western societies is to move away from traditional institution, including mainstream churches. An outcome of this process leads people to seek a sense of spirituality by themselves; they pick and choose what fits with their belief system. In this new diverse and multicultural era, people draw on a vast range of religious resources through consumerism. They will pray, meditate and read tarot cards. Crystals and icons will inspire them. They will visit churches and absorb themselves in nature. They will also find meaning through popular culture. They are looking for what works for them.

If this process is on one side of a spectrum, we find on the other side others for whom this world of choice might seem unbearable. Indeed, consumerism can be celebrated by some and disliked by others. While these less consumerist actors do not find answers in mainstream churches, they seek more "engaged" forms of religion (e.g. Pentecostalism) by looking for a stability of commitment in a community which would give a stronger sense of authority and a tighter system of beliefs and practices; that is, a more structured world/spiritual view. The way religious/spiritual actors deal with popular culture depends on what side of this heuristic spectrum they tend to be. On one end, we will see that there is a free-market consumption of popular culture as a source of spiritual/religious inspiration, whereas on the other side, this market still exists but is more restrictive – not in the quantity, but in the breadth of popular culture content – and even policed.

For a Weberian Approach

I do not intend to raise a critique of these religious/spiritual practices. My intention is to account for these practices and offer a fresh theoretical perspective that is inspired by the works of, for example, the postmodernists such as Baudrillard and Lipovetsky, and the critical theorists such as the Frankfurt School and Jameson.[1] Even if this book deals with postmodern practices, it does not follow a postmodernist approach. While it acknowledges the profound changes that have made our world

---

[1]   Although these perspectives seem contradictory in principle, Agger (1991) points out
their combined relevance when used by empirical sociologists.

postmodern, the underlying theoretical approach is Weberian. Weber believed that to understand a society, one needs to analyse the meaning social actors give to their action. Within this perspective, the sociologist is not simply a re-teller of social actors' stories. Rather, he or she is someone who uses his or her skills to understand a group of actors and uses his or her trained sociological imagination to put the actions of, and meanings given to these actions by, these social actors within a cultural context and structure.

After World War I, the Frankfurt school used Weber's work to adapt their Marxist perspective to the emergent consumer society. However this approach still remained within a perspective that viewed social actors as cultural dupes, controlled by the forces behind the emergence of mass consumption. This book, paradoxically, aims at re-adapting the theories of the Frankfurt School – and others such as Baudrillard – to a more Weberian approach which views social actors as agents, but still carried by some socio/cultural forces.

It is not the intention of this book to concentrate on the cultural content of popular culture only. Some popular works are blatantly religious, while many popular texts might have a dual nature; that is, a text and a sacred/divine subtext, or a narrative and a sacred/divine infranarrative. For example, Kozlovic (2003) researched many popular films and realised that Hollywood cinema very often employs, transforms and carries hidden sacred characters to spiritualise its "secular" products. This is not the aim of this book. The interest of this work lies more with a sociology of culture/religion than with an analysis carried in cultural analysis. The intention here is to study the impact these texts have on social actors, and vice versa. What is of interest is not if there is a religious/spiritual meaning in a text, but on why and how some social actors find a spiritual/religious meaning in a popular piece of work and what they do with it.

This book aims at taking the temperature of the times. Following the tradition of Simmel (1997) and Weber (1968), I am using a more impressionistic than positivist approach to articulate particular ideas from works of popular culture which in turn inform different religious values. As Street (1997: 147) argues, "no amount of empirical work will ever produce a definitive and irrefutable account of how exposure to popular culture produces particular results". However, there are elements scattered around in the information given by certain religious groups/actors and in various chat rooms on the Internet that inform us of a new trend in our postmodern societies.

The working assumption of popular culture is that it is a reflection of our society. The problem with this assertion is that the mirror is not always well polished. Images might sometimes be distorted, but there will always be an element of truth in them. Popular culture is part of consumer culture and we can know people by what they consume. Plato might have claimed the same if he were still alive. In his metaphor of the cave, prisoners are exposed to shadows that are distorting reality. These prisoners are chained and can only see the wall of the cave in which forms are reflected. They cannot perceive the fire behind them which creates these shadows. For Plato, popular culture would have been one of these projectors of shadows that would have reflected an obscure image of reality. For him, the only way to attain reality is to stop watching these shadows. Plato's eschatology is to see the light from the sun – that is getting out of the cave and seeing reality – by using philosophy and its structured reasoning. But what of our current world, so destroyed by postmodern philosophies that have moved away from this Platonic view to claim that "true" reality never existed? Nietzsche was one of the first to make such a claim. He argued that in a world in which nothing is real, one has to choose a "fake" moral of conduct which would be apt to the development of our individuality. For the German philosopher, if there is no reality, one can only lie to himself and herself when choosing a moral of conduct, and one can only grow stronger when acknowledging this. But what if popular culture is one of these lies? What if popular culture is used by people as a moral of conduct to direct people's lives in this postmodern world? In this world of choices, in which ideologies, religions and philosophies are on sale on the market of knowledge, can popular culture be found at the same level of quality? If for Nietzsche one has to lie to oneself by choosing a moral that views itself as real, how about a moral found in popular culture that has no pretension of being real?

By using this Weberian approach, I will argue that these new phenomena create new forms of religiosity adapted to our postmodern world. Since no "testament" has yet been written on this topic, this book views itself as the "hyper-real testament" (see Chapter 4) of these new religiosities.

Contents

To write such a testament, different gospels need to be told; these are listed below.

The first chapter, "Religion and Spirituality: From Modernity to Postmodernity", explores the shift from modernity to postmodernity which changed the religious landscape of western societies. A profound metamorphosis happened at the individual level which gives legitimacy to individuals to seek religious and spiritual content by themselves and for themselves. This seeking of content includes works of popular culture.

In Chapter 2, "Consumer Religion(s)", it is argued that all religions, whether they like it or not, are part of consumer society, but some are more consumerist – hyper consumerist religions – than others – hypo consumerist religions. It is revealed in this chapter that people in hyper consumer religions, according to Bauman, consume products for gaining and enhancing sensations. They can visit a "New Age" healing centre for a few days, participate in a "vision quest" and be initiated in shamanism, buy crystals, and indigenous paraphernalia, learn astrology… These objects for sale – books, tarot cards, crystals, CDs, aromatherapy products, etc. – have long lost any taint of the demonic and have become common products. This chapter underlines a strong correlation between these religions – e.g. "New Age" –, neo-liberal capitalism, and globalised consumer culture which has seen increasing prominence within (post)modern societies. However, this consumption of "sensations" is not restricted to commodities and services. It can be, following Mike Featherstone's work, extended to the consumption of signs and texts, and more specifically for this book to popular culture.

Chapter 3, "Subjective Myths", is an account of a new phenomenon in contemporary western society which appears to be saturated by media generated images of a "non-material", a de-materialised, concept of reality. According to Jean Baudrillard, we are now living in an economy of signs in which signs are exchanged against each other rather than against the real. From this, the real and unreal have imploded blurring the distinction between them and thus have become hyper-real. For example, religious doctrines and philosophies are mixed with conspiracy theories, alien intelligences, and Jedi religions; take for instance the groups who find inspiration for their spirituality from the stories of H.P. Lovecraft – Cthulhu mythos –, vampire stories, and the science fiction novel by Robert Heinlein (1987), *Stranger in a Strange Land* which inspired the Church of All Worlds. This chapter explores the eclectic consumption of popular culture which produces new and subjective myths in contemporary western culture; these are myths that have relevance to the self only.

The fourth chapter, "Hyper-Real Religion; e.g. *Star Wars*", follows closely the chapter on subjective myths, and analyses how religion can be created out of popular culture, thus becoming a hyper-real religion; that is, the simulacrum of a religion which provides inspiration for believers/consumers.

Chapter 5, "New Forms of Religious Identification Carried by Popular Culture", argues that popular culture can even offer support in forming new identities to groups and individuals who want to follow a religious and/or spiritual path. Indeed, in consumer culture, new identifications are being (re)created across the spheres of fiction and religion. This chapter investigates a case study by comparing the popularisation of the belief in the human potential ethic – i.e. the realisation of a "higher self" – found in alternative spiritualities with that of superheroes in comics. It will be shown that the popular growth of the belief in the human potential ethic and the development of superheroes in the comics' industry are in collusion – in Weber's sense – and offer a new choice of identification to consumers of popular culture. A comparison is also drawn with the power of the "Force" found in the *Star Wars* mythology.

In Chapter 6, "Esoteric Knowledge(s) and Popular Culture", it is observed that the blending of religion and popular culture can unintentionally affect certain forms of religion. This chapter explores the case study of esoteric knowledge, which seems no longer secret in western contemporary society; especially on the Internet. It is now part of popular and consumer culture and "secret wisdom" is no longer the privilege of an aristocracy of culture such as mystics or dervishes; it appears – paradoxically – to be within every individual's reach. Exploring this issue with the works of Simmel and Baudrillard, this chapter attempts 1) to understand the notion of secrecy, 2) to assess its place in popular and consumer culture – or what Baudrillard would call hyper-reality –, and 3) to evaluate the implication of this proliferation of "secret wisdom" in popular culture.

Chapter 7, "The Logic of Late Capitalism and the Stasis of Religion", brings previous argument into a new context. Following the work of Jameson, this chapter argues that certain forms of religion and popular culture are part of the logic of late capitalism; that is, the phase of late capitalism characterised by multinational corporations, its global market, and its mass consumption. Their interconnection creates new practices of religiosity never found in any previous society before. These new practices are part of what I call the "hyper-real testament". Paradoxically, since we have moved to postmodernism, the creation of new cultural content is in stasis and this can be applied to the field of religion. In terms of religious content, nothing new has been invented since the 1970s.

Chapter 8, "Popular Culture and Hypo-Consumer Religious Groups", goes deeply into the analysis of consumer culture by discovering that religious actors who express themselves in popular culture are also engaged in shaping popular culture, and in doing so, they make some experiences possible and deny access to others. This process can take the form of using the content of popular culture to back up their specific religion, or, it can take the form of censorship towards popular fictions. In this case, censorship produces a popular culture that profoundly affects what is heard and seen. The impact of new forms of religious fundamentalism(s) will be explored.

The conclusion explores the differences in the consumption of popular culture by hyper-consumer and hypo-consumer religions and, coming back to a Weberian approach, analyses these differences through the belief systems of these different consuming religions.

Note on Methodology

I conducted fieldwork in 1996-1997 that led to the submission of my doctoral thesis in 1998 at La Trobe University (Melbourne) which will be published as Possamai (forthcoming). This research dealt with New Age Spirituality and while conducting my interviews, I realised that there was a strong affinity between this spirituality and some forms of popular culture. This was a topic of research and analysis that had to be put on the side until this book. The interview extracts that are reproduced in parts in this book are from this fieldwork (see Chapter 2). Since my PhD, I have lectured in Sociology at the University of Western Sydney where I have been able to conduct more research on popular culture and other types of religions. As part of this research, I surfed on the Internet to discover relevant sites and analysed various chat rooms using a type of cyber-ethnography as detailed by Markham (1998). This method combines scholarly texts and narratives into a reflexive ethnography conducted at both the real and the virtual worlds. It aims to produce a type of anthropological/sociological "thick" description from which researches make claim, write case studies, and attempt to explain behaviour and attitude.

CHAPTER 1

Religion and Spirituality: From Modernity to Postmodernity

Introduction

Preacher is a graphic novel that pushes the boundaries of the imagination beyond heaven. The main character, Reverend Jesse Custer, is possessed by the entity Genesis – a child born of a union between an angel and a demon – and is on a quest to find God and the reason He has abandoned his post in heaven. Because of this symbiosis with this divine creature, Custer is able to speak with the voice of God and all he says has to be executed, even if this goes against one's will. On this quest, Tulip O'Hare, who was born with a gun on her hands, and Cassidy, a hard-drinking Irish vampire nearly a hundred years old, follow him. On their back is Grail, a centuries-old organisation controlling all world leaders. Grail has existed since the very beginning of our Christian era and has kept the bloodline of Jesus Christ intact. It is hiding the descendant of the Lord until the last one of the bloodline can be revealed on the day of the Apocalypse. By letting Jesus' children breed inside the same bloodline the world dominating organisation believes that the divine essence has never been tainted and the divine abilities of the son of God have remained within the descendant of Jesus. Starr, the order's most respected agent, is a far-right idealist who believes that democracy is for ancient Greeks and is a useless political ideal. He believes in Grail but not in the new Messiah. For many generations the descendants of Jesus have been born mentally ill, to the point of being completely debilitated. As he crudely states to one of his close men: "After two thousand years of keeping them breeding inside the one bloodline, we're lucky the bastard doesn't have antennae. [...] Son of God or son of man: you can't fuck your sister and expect too much good to come of it." For this reason, he is plotting to gain control of the organisation and use Jesse Custer's powers to turn the coming of the Apocalypse to Grail's advantage.

On the other hand, Custer is plotting against God and makes a pact with the Saint of Killers, an immortal gunfighter from the old American west who killed Satan many years ago. In the last volume of the series, the plot succeeds and the whole army of Angels from Heaven is completely destroyed by the guns of the Saint of Killers. When God finally comes back to his world, he is confronted with this killer who was patiently waiting for him sitting on Heaven's throne. The Saint, wanting to seek revenge from God who indirectly killed his wife and daughter when he was still a man, shoots him without any hesitation.

In this deistic and "roller coaster" reading of the world, God is finally dead. Grail, the most powerful religious group in the world, is destroyed and can no longer secretly govern the world. However, the magic and magical entities are still alive. In this narrative, organised forms of religions tend to be negatively portrayed whereas individual spiritually is perceived in a positive light. This trend can easily be found in other forms of popular culture. For example, McPhillips and Franzman (2000) and Clark (2003) discover that television series reflect current popular trends, e.g. towards denigration of institutionalized religions and uncritical acceptance of newer forms of religions. Traditional and institutional religions tend to be presented in a caricature form whereas newer forms of religions or spirituality are, in general, naïvely presented in a positive light.

Entertainment weekly described *Preacher* as featuring more blood and blasphemy than any mainstream comic in history.[1] While fans on the Internet find it provocative, atheists find it entertaining to see the traditional Christian mythologies turned upside down[2]. Curiously, using various web searches in March 2004, no reference to this graphic novel was found in any religious groups discussion on the Internet. However, what come out very quickly from an Internet search are the attacks on more innocent narratives from popular culture such as the Pokemon and Harry Potter. We will come back to this in Chapter 8.

One of the many underlying themes from this story about the preacher is that organised religions are no longer relevant and that individual spirituality is what matters the most. This tends to reflect much of today's concern in which believing without belonging (Davie, 1994) becomes more important. This chapter analyses the shift in people's perception of what is religious and what is spiritual. This shift does not happen in a religious/spiritual vacuum and is intrinsic to broader social and cultural changes. The following section analyses the dis-

---

[1]   Internet site, http//atheism.about.com/library/weekly/aa072298.htm (01/03/2004).

[2]   *O.c.*

placement of modernity to postmodernity to contextualise this change in the understanding of religion and spirituality.

Modernity and Postmodernity

For the purpose of this chapter, I will first detail two forms of rationality in the development of modernity, as formulated by Castoriadis (1992), and consider their involvement in postmodernity. I understand the terms modernity and postmodernity as ideal-types, or rather heuristic tools, which serve as a guide to understanding the interaction of broad cultural changes in western societies.

Castoriadis (1992: 18) defines modernity (1750-1950):

> by the fight, but also the mutual contamination and entanglement of these two imaginary significations: autonomy and unlimited expansion of "rational mastery". They coexist ambiguously under the common roof of "Reason".

"Rational mastery" is understood by the author as the living logic of capitalism. It is "embodied in quantification and lead[s] to the fetishization of growth" per se and its maximisation process treats other values such as human nature and traditions instrumentally. "Everything is called before the Tribunal of (productive) Reason and must prove its right to exist on the basis of the criterion of the unlimited expansion of 'rational mastery'" (*o.c.:* 19).

"Autonomy", on the other hand, is the critique of traditional and religious forces that held sway before the Enlightenment. This "reason" cleared the way for social and individual autonomy, i.e. "the affirmation of the possibility and the right for individuals and the collectivity to find in themselves (or to produce) the principle ordering their lives" (*o.c.:* 19).

For Castoriadis, these two "reasons" shared "the imaginary of Progress" and its technical-materialist utopia, and were in opposition and tension with one another. This conflict was the means of the dynamic development of western society and the expansion of capitalism.

Now, modernity is perceived as being in a crisis state. It is no longer a vehicle of ultimate meanings: the teleology of material progress proposed two centuries ago and increasingly accepted as common sense has lost its plausibility. Out of this loss, a reaction has appeared: postmodernism, "both as an effective historical trend and as a theory" (*o.c.:* 22).

Roseneau (1992: 127-133) shows us how, in the later twentieth century, critiques of modern reason, often seen as linked under the rubric of postmodernity, have diffused through western society. Included in these critiques is a questioning of universalist thinking concerning what is called "modernity", with a greater emphasis on feelings, emotions, intuition, creativity, imagination, fantasy, etc. together with a rejection of what was understood as the totalitarian and oppressive tendency of "Reason".

With the emergence of "Reason", human beings were expected to govern themselves in a civilised way. No longer were atrocious religious wars supposed to happen. However, the outcome of the development of "Reason" has not met its promises. We are now confronted with realities that we would have never expected in the time of Voltaire: the two World Wars, the rise of Nazism, the construction of concentration camps, various genocides, worldwide depression, Hiroshima, Vietnam, Cambodia, the Persian Gulf, a widening gap between rich and poor, and ecological catastrophes. All these atrocities are an outcome of the dream of "Reason", and this makes any contemporary belief in the ideology of progress questionable.

Bauman (1994) believes that modernity is no longer a force of liberation, but rather a source of oppression and repression. As he quotes Feingold (1983: 399-400) about the use of "Reason" with the holocaust:

[Auschwitz] was also a mundane extension of the modern factory system. Rather than producing goods, the raw material was human beings and the end-product was death, so many units per day marked carefully on the manager's production charts. The chimneys, the very symbol of the modern factory system, poured forth acrid smoke produced by burning human flesh. The brilliantly organised railroad grid of modern Europe carried a new kind of raw material to the factories. It did so in the same manner as with other cargo. In the gas chambers the victims inhaled noxious gas generated by prussic acid pellets, which were produced by the advanced chemical industry of Germany. Engineers designed the crematoria; managers designed the system of bureaucracy that worked with a zest and efficiency more backward nations would envy. Even the overall plan itself was a reflection of the modern scientific spirit gone awry. What we witnessed was nothing less than a massive scheme of social engineering [...]

Lyotard (1979), in his *Postmodern Condition*, theorises all ways of thinking and believing as narratives, i.e. the myriad stories or fables that we invent in order to give meaning and significance to our lives. These can be scientific, personal, mythical and religious. Lyotard uses a Nietzschean perspective and argues that there is no "Real" knowledge – i.e. a set of principles or beliefs that are intrinsically universal – and because of this, all narratives should be respected. However, certain narratives that emerged with modernity such as scientific knowledge and Marxism, portray themselves as universal and are called meta-narratives. The author warns us about these meta-narratives that make a false claim of universality, that we should be very sceptical about them. This sceptical attitude, or this crisis of knowledge, is what Lyotard calls the postmodern condition. In this condition, we should be cautious of the dominant use of "Reason" – called logocentrism – that tends to suppress and exclude all that which is different or does not fit with this universalising paradigm.

Castoriadis uses the work of Johann Arnason to summarise the theoretical or philosophical tenets of the present trend which undermine "modern reason".

1. The rejection of the global vision of history as progress or liberation.

2. The rejection of the idea of a uniform and universal reason.

3. The rejection of the strict differentiation of cultural spheres on the basis of a single underlying principle of rationality or functionality.

However, even if modernity's dream has faded, the belief in "rational mastery" is still alive and is no longer in tension with "Reason". But in as far as this development of capitalism has been decisively conditioned by the simultaneous development of the project of social and individual autonomy, modernity *is* finished. Capitalism developing whilst forced to face a continuous struggle against the *status quo*, on the floor of the factory as well as in the sphere of ideas or of art, and capitalism expanding without any effective internal opposition, are two different social-historical animals (Castoriadis, 1992: 23).

We will come back in Chapter 7 to "rational mastery" and its goal of unlimited capitalist expansion with the work of Jameson on the cultural logic of late capitalism and shed more light on this facet of postmodernity, religion and popular culture. However, for the remainder of this chapter, the focus will be on "Reason", starting first with its critique of traditional and religious forces.

Keeping Secularisation at Bay[3]

Part of this modernist project was the goal of keeping religion at bay. With the development of urbanism, science, mass education, etc., religion could no longer be the dominant force of western societies that guides people's thinking and actions. Ideologies in the name of "Reason" were attempting to supplant dominant religious views of the world

---

[3] For a recent and detailed account of the debate see for example, Lyon (2000), Dobbelaere (2002), or Beckford (2003).

by first hoping, like Comte, Marx and Freud, that it would completely disappear, or later, realising that it was not going away, by, at least, keeping religion outside of the public life and forcing it into the confined sphere of private life. Being religious in modernity was not about implementing new policies in parliament and/or working on new business deals in the name of God, but it was more about speaking about God at dinner table.

However, now that modernity is in crisis and that we are in the phase of postmodernity with its critique of logocentrism, secularisation theory appears now to be something of a "sacred canopy" (Richardson, 1985) for a majority of research in the social sciences of religion. Secularisation theory, not religion, now seems to be in crisis. Indeed, there is little dispute about one of the facts on which secularisation theory relied: that except for the USA (Warner, 1993), traditional institutional religion is in decline in modern society.

If traditional religious institutions have, in this perspective, lost their social significance, there are nevertheless still people feeling and confronting a religious experience they cannot always easily express. It appears that people still believe in God – or something or someone else – and feel they are confronting a religious world beyond church walls. One could recall that Troeltsch claimed in 1895 that religion was alive and abundant precisely because it was a time of ecclesial decline (Volker, 1997).

For Gauchet (1985), the Age of Religions as a structure is over, but it would be naive to believe that religion is over in terms of culture. This leads sociologists of religion to understand secularisation as the "privatisation of religion". Luckman (1967) discusses "invisible religion", a form of religiosity that has emerged in a period when the ecclesial religion was decaying, religion thus becoming a "private affair". As Beyer (1991) notes, this idea has been put forward by many sociologists since at least the 1960s, a time in which, for Casanova (1994), sociologists developed more systematic and empirically grounded theories of secularisation and distanced themselves from the past thesis that religion would eventually disappear from modern societies.

Kepel (1994) claims that if religion did become limited to the private sphere in a certain phase of modernisation in many societies around 1975, there was a reversal of this process around the world. Revived religious traditions no longer tried to adapt themselves to secular values but proposed alternative ways of organising society around sacred values. Kepel analyses some of these movements inside Judaism, Christianity and Islam and describes these religions as containing a high proportion of people who have a secular education but who want to submit reason to God's law. Following this line, Casanova (1994: 65-66) uses the term "deprivatization":

> the process whereby religion abandons its assigned place in the private sphere and enters the undifferentiated public sphere of civil society to take part in the ongoing process of contestation, discursive legitimation, and re-drawing of the boundaries.

The above emphasised that some politically and civil orientated re-ligions are now invading the public sector. This book will further the analysis of this re-invasion of religion in the public sphere by research-ing religions which are mainly orientated towards consumer culture – a dimension already touched by Eleta (1997) and her analysis of popular magic. As part of their involvement in consumer culture, religious groups promote their religious views through popular culture and occa-sionally attempt to police and control other views as well. The argument is not that these religions were created by consumer culture, but that they emerged and fully developed with the advent of this culture, and that through this process, they, in a way, became part of the mass me-dia.[4] The argument put forward is that even if consumerism has always been part of the field of religions in western history, it is only recently that it has emerged at a large scale. Some of these religions are individu-alistic and if they were not part of the ethos of pre-modern societies, they are now in full symbiosis with postmodern societies. Paradoxically, this became possible thanks to the works of some priests of secularism as explained in the next section.

The Secularist Break or the *Tertium Quid*

While modernist social engineers were working towards the control and containment, if not disappearance, of religion, new forms of religi-osities were seen as impossible to develop in such an atheistic environ-ment. Paradoxically, it can be argued that new forms of religiosities adapted themselves to, or were created within, modernity almost without being wounded by the dialectic between advocates of secularism and the Church, or what Russell (1960: 171) presents as the warfare between science and theology. Of course, the actual debate between scientists and theologians is much more complex and subtle than the image of two-sided warfare allows. But perhaps there is enough reality in it to allow a point to be made.

---

[4] The study of mass media argues against the distinction of the private and public spheres (see e.g. Rosenau (1992: 101). If we can argue that religion has some strong links with popular culture and the mass media, we could argue in a sense, that relig-ion might still be part of the public sphere at a cultural level.

The point is, that while there was what I call a secularist break between scientific reason and ecclesial religion, these new religiosities became a site of contestation for actors less involved in the big conflict. In this triangle, these religiosities were a *tertium quid*[5] which (if I may caricature) was left alone by its two opponents and enabled to flourish.

This development in the secularist break of modernity is consistent with the view of Stark and Bainbridge (1985: 441-442) who argue that:

> [...] centuries of secularization have made ruins of many of the traditional religious bodies. But the process of secularization has not caused people to reject the possible existence of supernatural forces or caused them no longer to desire things that are difficult or impossible to obtain in this world.

One of the main assumptions from these authors is that cults – i.e. new forms of religions – flourish where the conventional churches are weakest:

> What organizational secularization has produced is a large population of unchurched people who retain their acceptance of the existence of the supernatural. They seem only to have lost their faith in the ability of the conventional churches to interpret and serve their belief in the supernatural. Hence, it should be no surprise that many of these unchurched believers are willing, perhaps eager, to examine new religions, to find a faith that can offer an active and vigorous conception of the supernatural that is compatible with modern culture (*o.c.*: 444).

The metaphor of religious economy helps us make the same point. For this, Stark and Iannaccone (1994) argue that the capacity for a simple religion to monopolise a religious economy depends "upon the degree to which the State uses coercive force to regulate the religious economy" (*o.c.*: 232), and "[t]o the degree that a religious economy is unregulated, it will tend to be very pluralistic" (*ibid.*). Indeed, Christian churches lost their religious monopoly during modernity, and this religious economic deregulation has permitted other "religious firms" – to use the authors' concept – to offer their religious products.[6] Further, the move to postmodernity has made our society so pluralistic and multilayered that we can now more appreciate Durkheim's prediction that "a highly specialised and diversified society will produce highly specialised, diversified and individualistic religion" (Westley, 1978: 137).

---

[5] *Tertium Quid*: "some third thing [...]. Something (indefinite or left undefined) related in some way to two (definite or known) things, but distinct from both! (*The Shorter OED*, 3rd edition, Oxford, Oxford University Press, 1973).

[6] Another factor is denominationalism, i.e. a social psychology of the pluralistic culture which diminishes any dogmatism (See Bruce, 1996).

Secularisation – if I may caricature and omit other factors – at once made redundant a coercive power or a monopolised religious economy and gave to new religiosities the opportunity to emerge from their "discreet" refuges. This deregulation has been seen by Beckford (2003) as one of the hidden ironies of secularisation.

Using either set of organising concepts, we are now in a position to appreciate Colin Campbell's conclusion:

[...] we can now consider the general thesis that the overall processes of secularization, insofar as these can be successfully discerned, have had a differential impact upon religion, and that while they seem by and large to have worked to the disadvantage of church religion (and to a lesser extent sect religion) they have actually favoured the growth of spiritual and mystical religion in the modern world. [...] This form of religion has thus prospered at the expense of the others because it is better adapted to survive in a scientific, secular culture. The characteristics which give mystical religion its adaptive advantage in this sense are its monism, relativism, tolerance, syncretism, and above all, its individualism (C. Campbell, 1978: 152-153).

Religion and Spirituality

What is meant by being religious today is no longer what it once was.[7] Religion is metamorphosing into new, re-newed and different forms at various levels (Lyon, 2000). As a result of the collapse of collective systems of codes and being, the result is an increase of freedom in which the individual makes his or her own sense of his or her life and of the rapid changes specific to our current society. More people claim to have no religious affiliations but they are not necessarily atheist; they believe without belonging and might see themselves as more spiritual than religious. In everyday life/language, religion appears to be connected with institutionalised/organised forms whereas spirituality is viewed more as a self-authored search by individuals who are looking inward.[8] With secularization, the cultural presence of traditional religious institutions has diminished, but the search for a more personal connection to a religion, that is, for spirituality, has increased. In various surveys (Marler and Hadaway, 2002; Hugues *et al.*, 2003), we see that the younger the generation the more spiritual (only) rather than religious it is.

---

[7] Even if there is a difficulty in defining what religion was and is (see for example Berger, 1974, and Beckford, 2003), it can nevertheless be argued that there has been a change of perception.

[8] Indeed, we will see in Chapter 3 how the shift to postmodernity has increased the importance of the self.

Sociologists have suggested that "spirituality" might have replaced "religion", as the term seems more adequate to the current religious quest in consumer culture (e.g. Roof, 1999).[9] However, recent research (e.g. Marler and Hadaway, 2002; Hugues *et al.*, 2004) indicates that spirituality is not simply replacing religion. Most people see themselves as "religious" and "spiritual" at the same time. In a survey that Marler and Hadaway (2002) conducted in 1999, differences in the ways those terms are used and understood can be found.

Table 1. Being Religious and Being Spiritual by Age Cohort in the United States, 1991 (Percentage in each Age Cohort)

	Oldest	Born 1927-1945	Baby Boomers	Baby Busters
Religious and spiritual	66.8	67.1	64.9	54.9
Spiritual only	14.5	16.7	19.8	22.6
Religious only	11.0	8.9	8.0	8.3
Neither	7.7	7.3	7.2	14.2
N	*310*	*496*	*761*	*288*

Source: Marler and Hadaway (2002: 293).

In Australia, albeit a slight difference between age groups, Hughes *et al.* (2004) discover similar trends to the research above.

Table 2. Being Religious and Being Spiritual by Age Group in Australia, 2002 (Percentage in Each Age Group)

	70 plus	60 to 69	50 to 59	40 to 49	30 to 39	18 to 29
"Religious" and "spiritual"	40.5	50.6	36.2	41.3	34.3	34.0
Spiritual only	2.6	3.8	11.4	9.1	9.1	11.5
Religious only	19.8	11.4	13.4	8.4	8.8	5.3
Neither	37.1	34.2	39.0	41.3	47.9	49.2
N	*116*	*158*	*254*	*383*	*353*	*191*

Source: Hugues *et al.* (2004)

These researchers have also been able to show that being spiritual does not necessarily mean not being religious. For example, Wuthnow (2001: 307) claims that "many people who practice spirituality in their

---

[9] It is interesting to note that the word "spirituality" was first used in the seventeenth century as a pejorative term to refer to elite forms of individual religious practice (Cunningham & Egan, 1996: 5).

own ways still go to church or synagogue". From a Christian perspective, Cunningham and Egan (1996) make reference to spirituality as the
lived encounter with Jesus Christ in the Spirit. For them, spirituality
cannot be limited to an exclusively individualistic "care of the soul" and
involves being part of the local and worldwide community. Going to
"church" on Sunday allows this connection, and furthermore, by listening to the word of God, Christians can enter "into the story that tells us
about Jesus the Christ in the Spirit [i.e. being spiritual] and to respond to
that story both as individuals and as part of the local and worldwide
community" (*o.c.*: 33). Indeed, social scientists find from various surveys that the large majority of the people surveyed claim to be religious
and spiritual at the same time, whereas those who claim to be spiritual
but not religious appear to be only a small contingent of people, and
spirituality does not seem to replace religion at all. These spiritual (only)
actors are not churchgoers and are more likely to be agnostic who
experiment with alternative spiritualities and/or Eastern practices. From
such research, it appears that there are two types of spiritual actors, the
one that claims that he or she is still religious – the majority according
to the two tables above –, and the one that is not religious. To make
sense of this, it is worth coming back to the classics to put some light on
this contemporary phenomenon. Troeltsch's work on mysticism has
some strange resemblances with the contemporary spiritual trend.

Bruce Campbell (1978: 231) quotes Troeltsch's definition of mysticism as

> the insistence upon a direct inward and present religious experience. [...] An
> individualised reaction against highly institutionalised religion, it arises
> when "the world of ideas" which makes up the religious belief system has
> "hardened" into formal worship and doctrine. Under these circumstances,
> religion becomes for some people "transformed into a purely personal and
> inward experience".

The author gives a summary of the characteristics of Troeltsch's
mysticism as "an emphasis on direct, inner personal experience; loose
and provisional forms; voluntary adherence, usually not formal; a
spiritual conception of fellowship; inclusiveness in attitude; indifference
toward the demands of society" (*o.c.*: 231). Nelson (1987: 56) also adds
that mystics, even if they go through a religious individuation process,
get together and do not stay alone in their spiritual ivory tower. They
form organisations because of the need they feel for the give and take of
intimate fellowship with their religious peers.

B. Campbell (1978: 231) and Garret (1975: 215) have found that
Troeltsch writes about two ideal-types of mysticism; these are mysticism and technical mysticism.

1– Mysticism occurs in established religious traditions but its experience occurs outside the regular forms of worship and devotion to these religions. The experience of the mystics, from this ideal-type, is the means by which they realise and appropriate the tradition of the religious organisation in which they belong. They do not detract from the existing sociological forms of religion even if mysticism embodies the form of the highest religious individualism (Bastide, 1996: 197-206). They even legitimise and support established ecclesiastical structures.

2– Technical mysticism makes a break with traditional religion. Technical mystics contest the religion within which they have been socialised. They understand themselves to be independent from religious principle, independent of every religious institution and reject the religious morality they have received *cum lacte*.[10] Technical mysticism sets up its own theory, which takes the place of doctrine and dogma by undercutting the form and structure of the established religions. It discovers everywhere, "beneath all the concrete forms of religion, the same religious germ [...]" (Troeltsch, 1950: 231).

This technical mysticism in the narrower sense, with its own philosophy of religion, has also appeared in various religious spheres with a remarkable similarity of form: in Indian Brahmanism and its repercussion in Buddhism, in the Sufism of the Parsees and of Persian Muslims, in the Neo-Platonism of the Greeks, in the varied syncretism of late Antiquity which is known as Gnosticism (*o.c.*: 736).

As Garret (1975: 215-126) realises, mysticism and technical mysticism are far from being a unitary phenomenon. The sociological consequences springing from these two analytical sub-types press in antithetical directions: the one legitimating ecclesial structures, the other innovating new forms of religions.

Could it be argued that those surveyed and claiming to be spiritual and religious would be mystical in Troeltsch's understanding, and that those claiming to be spiritual but not religious are technical mystics? There are indeed clear similarities that can help us with the argument of this book. It is thus tempting to call those who claim to be spiritual and religious as spiritual, and those who are spiritual only as technical spiritual. I would like to point out that I do not equate being spiritual with being mystic. I am simply arguing that there are strong sociological resemblances between these two ideal-types of actors and that Troeltsch's typology could be usefully translated to the current research on spirituality. By ideal type, I make reference to a typification method, which stresses, links and organises the traits that are common to a

---

[10] As the Romans used to say: "with mother's milk".

specific category of phenomena in an ideal category that does not necessarily fully represent reality.

Among these spiritual actors, there are of course many different levels of individualism within an organised religion; however, there are elements of individualism. The distinction between these two types of spiritual actors will be helpful in understanding their level of religious consumption in the next chapter. It will be argued that those involved in – what I will call hyper-consumer religions (e.g. New Age) – are techno-spiritual actors.

Troeltsch claimed that mysticism and technical mysticism were, at the beginning of the twentieth century, the secret religion of the educated class, and predicted that gradually, in the world of "mass" educated people, this type of religiosity would be predominant. C. Campbell (1978) saw this in the late 1960s and early 1970s with the development of new religious movements as prescient. It is even more prescient today, at the beginning of the twenty-first century, in which spirituality has become so important and so mainstream.

Conclusion

Coming back to the secularisation debate, it is worth emphasising Dobbelaere's (2002) analysis. He considers the process of secularisation as having three levels, however, the one that concerns us for the moment is what he calls the individual secularisation. By this, he does not make reference to an eclipse of religion/spirituality from the life of the individual but to individuals who "have liberated themselves from religious authorities and that their experiences are the basis of their faith" (*o.c.*: 190):

> [...] individual secularization is not only about *decline* of religiosity, it is also about *changes, shifts, or transformations of the authority structure of the beliefs and practices* one holds: from church authorities to the self and his or her experiences, which is clearly indicated by the growing use of the term "spirituality" instead of "religiosity" or "religiousness" to label one's faith (*o.c.*: 178).

This individual secularisation is an outcome of what he calls the societal secularisation – i.e. "a process by which the over-arching and transcendent religious system of old is being reduced in modern functionally differentiated societies to a sub-system alongside other sub-systems losing in this process its overarching claims over the other sub-systems" (*o.c.:* 189) – that is, a consequence of the development of modernity. With individual secularisation, many social actors claim to be spiritual but not religious or to be spiritual and religious, and are active in this field. Recent research in Australia (Bouma and Lennon, 2003) indicates that ten percent of households report taking part in religious/spiritual activities on an average day, and that these activities represent 0.28 percent of all activities. The rating of these activities do not rate with eating, sleeping or watching TV, however, they have a similar rate to engaging in sporting and cultural activities.

As part of these changes in the way(s) of being religious/spiritual, this book argues that reading, watching and listening to popular culture has also become a spiritual activity for some social actors. If watching TV in Australia is a more important activity than practising one's religion, some of the shows and movies can provide a source of spiritual inspiration. We will come back to this after analysing the impact of consumerism – from which popular culture is an important part – on religion.

CHAPTER 2

Consumer Religions

Introduction

In the movie *Dogma*, a Catholic priest has firmly decided to bring the flock back to church. Looking like a kind of general-priest who has had the rough experience of fighting in the front line, he is ready to launch a marketing war. His task is not an easy one. To reach his aim, he decides to move the "atavistic" church to contemporary consumer culture and thus market his faith with the sign of the times. One of his first actions is to uncover a new image of the Christ at a press conference in front of his urban church. The old imagery of the Christ suffering on the cross and dying for our sins, no longer fits with a society of leisure in which suffering and pain are not well marketed. In a consumer society that holds people together, not as citizens but as consumers, the majority of people are more interested in a religious quick fix than to follow a long journey of spiritual pain/gain. The Priest then gets rid of the cross, the Christian symbol of torture, puts an inviting smile on the face of Jesus, and places him in a thumb up gesture to give him a more welcoming posture. The new representation of Christ is now called the "Buddy Christ" and is everyone's friend; exactly like the McDonald's clown. With this new marketing device, the Priest is now ready to compete with other religions and bring believers back.

From this example from popular culture, we can touch on some difficulties that traditional religions are faced by our current consumerist world and how they have to modify themselves to fit with our *Zeitgeist*. On the other hand, new forms of religions seem to emerge with the spirit of our time and are fully adapted to it, such as the commonly called New Age spiritualities. This chapter will argue that even if all forms of religions are affected by these socio-cultural changes that make our society a consumerist one, some are more integrated than others. Popular culture in western society is part of this consumer culture, however, we will only focus on that aspect in the next chapter.

41

Consumption

Consumption for leisure and lifestyle was only restricted to a few groups within the dominant class until the advent of mass consumption. Now, all people from all wages who are included in this society take part in it – those who do not take part, the non-consumers, are simply excluded.

Indeed, for Bauman (1998), a "normal life" in a consumer society is the life of consumerism which involves making choices among all the displayed opportunities. A "happy life" is then defined as taking as many opportunities as possible. The poor in consumer society is not necessarily the one who does not have a shelter but is the one who has no access to a normal life and to a "happy" one. To be one of these is then to be a consumer *manqué*. As Bauman (1998: 38) explains:

> In a society of consumers, it is above all the inadequacy of the person as a consumer that leads to social degradation and "internal exile". It is this in-adequacy, this inability to acquit oneself of the consumer's duties, that turns into bitterness at being left behind, disinherited or degraded, shut off or ex-cluded from the social feast to which others gained entry. Overcoming that consumer inadequacy is likely to be seen as the only remedy – the sole exit from a humiliating plight.

Consumer culture is the outcome of the massive expansion of the production of capitalist commodity. This outburst of the capitalist system has created a vast reservoir of consumer goods and sites for purchase and consumption to be "enjoyed" by the various classes of our society that are "in". This has lead to the growing dependence on mass leisure and consumption activities. This is viewed by some as leading to more egalitarianism and individual freedom (e.g. De Certeau, 1988) and by others as an increase in the ideological and seductive manipulation of the masses by the dominant class. This manipulation would distract the masses from considering an alternative to our society which could improve our social relations (e.g. the Frankfurt School).

Whatever the perspective taken, it cannot be denied that leisure has been commercialised. No longer is it a communal form of play; it is now a commercial form of entertainment. For example, Langer (1996) discovers that birthday parties have become part of this process. Few people in their seventies and eighties would have had celebrated their birthday as children. The first generation to start celebrating this event were the baby boomers. This new way of celebrating someone's birth has even paved the way for mass production of cheap toys. However, these birthday parties were organised at home and entertainment often involved cheap games. In the 1980s and 1990s, birthday parties became part of a service industry. McDonalds, Pizza Hut, Pancake Parlour, and Timezone now offer special "party packages" with specialists – e.g. party coordinator, caterers and clown – to take care of the event; and it becomes hard to refuse one of these parties to a child under peer pressure. This industrialisation of birthday parties even turns children's parties into an opportunity for "conspicuous consumption", i.e. the competitive display of capacity to spend money on inessentials.

When Baudrillard (1970) was a Marxist, before his move towards postmodernism (see Chapter 4), he viewed pleasure as being constrained and institutionalised. It is no longer a wish or a desire to just have fun; it is almost a citizen's duty to take part actively in consumer culture. The masses are being socialised into a force of consumption and must learn how to live the pleasure offered by this culture. In this perspective, there is an increase from production society to consumer society for the capacity for ideological manipulation by a type of corporate capitalism.

This view is similar to that of the Frankfurt School which understands the proletariat as a socially impotent force that has lost its revolutionary role. Capitalism has managed to create a society of compliant workers and consumers. This school of thought also coined the concept of "culture industry" to shed more light on this process. The term was introduced by Max Horkheimer and Theodor Adorno in the 1940s to argue that the arts were no longer independent of industry and commerce. In this culture industry, industrial manufacturing, commerce and artistic endeavour have been fusioned in such a way that there now remains no difference between companies producing hit songs or movies and the industries that manufacture vast amounts of mass-produced foods, clothing and automobiles. If I may overly generalise, no longer do we have the artist-hero as a genius who is ready to starve – or cut off his ear – for the sake of his or her art. Now, the artist is not necessarily a genius but more of a cultural worker (see Chapter 7). Culture is no longer the preserve of the artist; it is now adapted to methods used in industrial manufacturing and in marketing.

Schiller (1996: 114) brings this concept up-to-date and alerts us to how, since the globalisation of communication in the 1960s, we have seen the growth of transnational media-information corporations such as Time Warner, Disney, Reuters, Sony and Murdoch's News Corporation. As he claims (1996: 114):

> [...] a world-class cultural industry corporation such as Time Warner or Disney, or one of Murdoch's enterprises, can combine a rich mix of information, pop-cultural activities, synergistically spinning one product off another, or promoting one item by incorporating it in another format. TV pro-

grams and movies are retailed as video cassettes and their sound tracks move out into their own orbits as records and tapes. To top it off, sophisticated management of a conglomerate like Disney, engages as well in retail business, selling its various creations and promotions that originated as film or television, in shops owned or franchised.

A more recent phenomenon of this cultural industry is the close link between Hollywood and the computer game industry. According to Williams (2003), video games grossed more than the cinema in 2002 in the USA. Furthermore, the computer technologies used to create both movies and games are moving closer and closer together. For example, Tobey Maguire and Willem Dafoe, while filming Spiderman, were asked to visit the computer game studio to have their faces scanned so the characters in the games would look more realistic. As the producer of the movie, Brian Pass, states: "I definitely see a time when you are not going to be able to see a difference between what's been rendered out of a games console and what's happening in a film" (Williams, 2003).

However, if we come back to a more positive view on consumer culture (e.g. De Certeau), and we move away from thinking of ourselves as part of the "inactive mass", we can think of consumers as active agents who create their own identity through consumption. In this case, they are creating a bricolage – literally the activity of self-consciously mixing and matching any disparate elements that may be at hand – which can produce new cultural identities by cutting across social divisions. In this perspective, all consumer behaviour becomes almost imbued with a romantic glow of creativity.

In his analysis of capitalism, De Certeau argues that workers are involved in what he calls "*La Perruque*". In French, it means "The Wig", and in the author's language, it is the worker's own work disguised as work for his employer; that is, a diversionary practice. This practice can simply be an office worker writing a love letter on "company time", a factory worker borrowing tools and raw material to build something for his home, an IT officer playing a game, a secretary sending personal e-mails, or an academic reading a graphic novel in his office – *mea culpa*. This practice diverts time that is free, creative and not directed towards profit. The same can be applied to consumer culture, in which consumers divert the original intention of the producers and consume for their own pleasure. For example, Fiske (1989) analyses shopping malls and realises that if their architecture and structure are designed in such a way as to convince people to buy without thinking twice, there are youth groups who appropriate the space from the mall to their advantage. They use this environment for leisure with their friends without having to consume more than necessary. The same goes for people who learn about the good deals offered in the mall and thus take advantage of the system.

Within this perspective on consumer culture, it can be argued that mass society does not necessarily oppress individuals as the Frankfurt School would like us to think, but that it might be liberating people by offering multiple avenues for individual expressions through a range of commodities which can be appropriated by the individual and worked into their own specific style.

This section has given a quick background on the theories of consumer culture and many more detailed theoretical accounts will be presented in the chapters to come. However, before refining our epistemological view, it is necessary to come back to the field of religion.

Religion and Consumption

Ritzer (1999) makes reference to new means of consumption – e.g. malls, superstores, airports, and cruise ships – as "cathedrals of consumption". These cathedrals, in order to attract a larger amount of customers, need to offer a magical, fantastic and enchanting shopping environment.[1] For example, shopping malls can be interpreted as places where people practice their "consumer religions":

> Malls provide the kind of centeredness traditionally provided by religious temples, and they are constructed to have similar balance, symmetry, and order. Their atriums usually offer connection to nature through water and vegetation. People gain a sense of community as well as more specific community services. Play is almost universally part of religious practice, and malls provide a place for people to frolic. Similarly, malls offer a setting in which people can partake in ceremonial meals. Malls clearly qualify for the label of cathedrals of consumption. (*o.c.*: 9)

Although it can be claimed that the cathedrals of consumption have a quasi religious character, some religious groups are specifically following and promoting the consumerist aspect of these cathedrals.

For example, Trueheart (1996) writes about the Next Church, also called mega churches, full-service churches, seven-day-a-week churches, pastoral churches, apostolic churches, "new tribe" churches, new paradigm churches, seeker-sensitive churches, or shopping-mall churches. The Next Church, at least in its American context, transcends denominations and the traditional way of attending a church. It is evangelical and

---

[1] See for example Langer's (2004) analysis of the toy industry in which "the magic of childhood" and its world of imagination is being used to "enchant" the market.

tends to be Christian literalist. Under one roof, these churches offer pop-culture packaging worship styles to boutique ministries. The latest generation has huge auditoriums and balconied atriums, orchestras and bands playing soft rock, some of them with even food courts, fountains, "plus plenty of parking, clean bathrooms, and the likelihood that you'll find something you want and come back again" (*o.c.:* 49):

> Growing churches and congregations, like growing businesses, have a reflexive thirst for market share. They tend to equate rising numbers with self-worth and bricks and mortar with godliness. But growth is also an expression of the evangelical mission. When I marvelled to Bill Hybels, of Willow Creek, about his church's phenomenal growth and size – more than 15,000 attend a worship service every weekend – he frowned. "There are two million people within a one-hour drive of this place", he said. "In business parlance, we've got two percent of market share. We've got a long way to go".
> (*o.c.:* 52)

Ritzer (1999: 6) quotes the analogy of the "Wal-Mart-ization of American Religions" and a pastor of a large Baptist church hoping to turning his services into a "fun" event asked his staff to study Disney World. Following the work of Ritzer on his work on the McDonaldization of society – that is "the process by which the principles of the fast food restaurant are coming to dominate more and more sectors of American society as well as the world" (Ritzer, 2000) – Drane (2000) argues that the church follows this process and offers uninventive pre-packaged worship and theology.[2]

In a recent report from Wayne Brighton, a researcher with the General Synod Office of the Anglican Church, it is revealed that the Church has been recommended to have a more community-based approach, including café churches (Price, 2004). The Café churches are organised to have people sitting at tables and chairs, drinking and/or eating and chatting. By using a style of sociation more appropriate to our consumer society than having people preached at from a pulpit, it is hoped to increase church attendance. This would have already been endorsed by the Church of England in Britain.

Another phenomenon is that of electronic churches (Lyon, 2000: 62-66) which have shifted the church attendants from the church pews to their own sofa in front of their television. Billy Graham and Jim Bakker, for example, employed a "religious industry" to extend their evangelism through the television media. These televangelists represent different

---

[2] Drane (2000) uses this analogy to illustrate one of the reasons why the churches are struggling to maintain credibility. A large part of his book is informing the church-worker that the churches need to reconnect to their creativity and flexibility to reach post-modern spiritual actors.

religious orientations and even if they tend to be politically conservative, only a few are reactionary fundamentalists.

Religion in our postmodern times – whether we like or not – is definitely part of consumer culture. All religious groups produce commodities, or put positive values in some commodities, that can be bought by the religious consumer. Some groups are more involved than others and can vary from Hare Krishna devotees selling books at a stall at a university campus or selling vegetarian meals in a restaurant, to Christian shops selling books and other artefacts, to the Church of Scientology asking for a fee for each level of spiritual development, or to New Age shops offering anything that can help the spiritual actor on his or her quest. It cannot be claimed that religion has always been protected from consumer culture until now – one can remember Jesus protesting against the merchants in the Temple. However, what is new is religion's full immersion into it; some groups celebrating it, others resisting certain aspects of it. It becomes almost a truism to state that for a group to spread its beliefs and values, it now has to speak a language that the majority of people can understand: that of consumption. For example, Robyn and Roger organise "New Age" festivals in the hope that some ideas will stay in the minds of the people wandering past the displays:

> Robyn: The general people who are searching, even though it's not getting them into the depth of it, but it's obvious that they come to this [New Age festival] because they're searching for something within themselves. And even though you present it in a light, fantastic way and fantasy and fun, there is a depth I believe.
>
> Roger: Definite resonance. Going on within the world.
>
> Robyn: Yes, within them. And that's why they come along. And we have good you know happy people.
>
> Roger: Good vibes.
>
> Robyn: Good vibes yeah. And they go away and even if, you say, did you have a good day, "Oh we had a lovely day thank you". But they don't understand the depth of the meaning of what's happened to them, there's something stirring within them. [...] The New Age festivals just get them going and it's up to the person.
>
> Roger: It's a catalyst. It brings it all together.
>
> Robyn: Yes. It just made good some spark in them that gets them going.
>
> Roger: Inspiration.
>
> Robyn: Yes. That's what I believe.
>
> Roger: Even if for some people it will remain out of their conscious awareness, they won't quite understand, remain unconscious, and it gives them some inspiration. Some sort of stimulation.

Robyn: Yes. Something gets into their subconscious there.

Roger: That's right.

As Robyn and Roger remind us, there is a production of symbols in "New Age" festivals that, according to them, stays in the mind of the religious consumer and may affect his or her beliefs – though the extent of this effect remains unknown.

Post war consumer culture dominates the western lifestyle with its mass produced commodities and western culture. This culture, instead of building a sense of belonging for groups – e.g. class, sub-cultures, political parties – appears to create a fragmented society in which religion is only a part. Indeed, in this consuming world, the individual becomes his or her own authority; the postmodern person in the West no longer tolerates being told what to believe and what to do. Consumer choice is not limited to shopping, but is extended to education, health, politics and religion. People are now "free to choose" and the market culture might be turning us into consumers rather than citizens (Lyon, 2000:12). He or she is faced with a proliferation of "spiritual/religious/philosophical knowledges", which he or she researches and experiences.

Sometimes, as found in many New Age spiritualities, this religious choice is celebrated; sometimes this choice is a burden of responsibility too heavy for a religious consumer. To this burden, fundamentalism seems to offer a solution. Fundamentalism, according to Bauman (1998: 72), is a postmodern phenomenon, supporting the "rationalising, reforms and technological development of modernity". They offer a full enjoyment of today's development without paying a heavy price; the price of self-sufficiency, self-reliance and a feeling of never being fully satisfied.

If market-type rationality is subordinated to the promotion of freedom of choice and thrives on the uncertainty of choice-making situations, the fundamentalist rationality puts security and certainty first and condemns everything that undermines that certainty – the vagaries of individual freedom first and foremost (*o.c.:* 75).

Apart from various forms of fundamentalism, which we will analyse in detail in Chapter 8, and which are a response to a choice-overload within consumer societies (Bauman, 1998), it can be argued that all religions are part of consumer culture, but some are more involved than others. In Zaidman (2003), we are given a comparison between traditional and New Age religion in regards to the commercialisation of religious objects. The findings are based on fieldwork in Israel with pilgrims visiting saints' tombs. While both groups are part of consumer culture, a difference is found in regards to participants' perspectives on "the commercialisation of religious goods, the role of marketing agents, and the general characteristics of the market" (Zaidman, 2003: 357). In traditional religions, the demand for religious objects is focused on their authenticity. New objects will not be bought unless there is proof that they are authentic for a specific religion, and that they contain the power of a specific source. In New Age, the individual is the main source of meaning attribution, and the authority of the object rests in the individual's decision and/or feeling about the worth of its religiousness. In New Age, spiritual actors will seek expanding markets and new sources of religious goods.

From this research, it can easily be inferred that religious consumers are active in different religious groups; however, the point here is to distinguish these styles of consumption. The religious belief will canvass the consumer's choice. In some religious forms, the consumer is his or her own authority in deciding what to consume, in others, there is a reliance on a guidance that justifies the religious values of these commodities. It could be argued that in postmodern times, we have two extremes. On the one hand, New Age spiritualities are perceived as having no boundaries in their consumption, on the other hand, consumers from some religious groups need to be guided by a recognised authority. In between these two extremes of a continuum, we find all other religious groups. This book will mainly deal with these two extremes of this continuum and offer two extreme views on the consumption of religion – including the consumption of popular culture. New Age spiritualities can be seen as the hyper-consumerist religion whereas fundamentalism can be seen as the hypo-consumerist religion. There is consumption on both ends, but on one hand, there is a celebration of choice by the individual, on the other, there is a control of choice by a recognised authority. This book will now deal with this hyper-consumerist aspect until Chapter 7. In Chapter 8, we will come back to the hypo-consumerist religions.

It can thus easily be argued that New Age is the consumer religion *par excellence,* which is the focus of the following sections.

Hyper-Consumer Religions

People involved in alternative spiritualities are part of what Bauman (1998) calls postmodern religions, and more specifically "consumer religions". They consume products for gaining and enhancing sensations. They can visit a "New Age" healing centre for a few days, participate in a "vision quest" and be initiated in shamanism, buy crystals and indigenous paraphernalia, learn astrology... These objects for sale – books, tarot cards, crystals, CDs, aromatherapy products, etc. – have long lost any taint of the demonic and have become common products. "New Age" festivals and psychic fairs proliferate. Consultants, tarot card readers, clairvoyants and so on, offer their services not only in specialist shops and fairs, but also in more conventional shops – like craft shops and galleries – and craft markets as well as from private homes. Many conventional book and music shops often have a stall specifically for "New Age" books and recordings. An array of popular journals, magazines and fanzines diffuse "New Age" discourses. In the USA, there are 100 "New Age" magazines and also "New Age" radio stations (Heelas, 1993: 112). These practices and beliefs are part of what Eleta (1997) terms "popular magic", and, according to her, have become a consumer product in contemporary society. Studies by Heelas (1993), Roberts (1994), Hill (1992), Van Hove (1999) and York (1999) under-line a strong correlation between "New Age", neo-liberal capitalism, and globalised consumer culture which has seen increasing prominence within (post)modern societies.[3] However, this consumption of "sensa-tions" is not restricted to commodities and services. It can be, following Featherstone's (1991) work, extended to the consumption of signs and texts, and more specifically to signs and texts found in indigenous culture, history (this chapter) and popular culture (next chapter). This will be addressed after investigating these so-called "New Agers".

Who are these religious and consuming actors? In 1996-1997, I in-terviewed 35 people from Melbourne who would "commonly" be described as New Agers. They were involved in practices such as astrol-ogy, automatic writing, (western) Buddhism, channelling, crystals manipulation, feminist spirituality, meditation, naturopathy, numerol-ogy, palmistry, Reiki, spiritualism, Tantrism, tarot cards, and urban shamanism. However, 25 (71%) of the participants criticised New Age, and 3 (9%), even if they were not opposed to it, did not consider them-selves as New Agers. Three of the many negative comments were:

> It's like a train labelled New Age and everybody's jumping on it. And it started off very good, a very good term. But now there's a lot of people out trying to make big money on it for all the wrong reasons.

> So I guess I'm a bit of a, you know I'm not your typical New Age, totally im-mersed in it sort of person [...]. I mean my personal feeling is that I like to keep my feet on the ground a bit [...].

> They're [New Agers] looking for an answer and they want a quick easy one. There are no quick easy answers so they'll fake it [...] well, they're weird but they're mostly harmless.

---

[3] However, Heelas (1993) also refers to another wing of "New Age" that is not involved in pro-capitalism, is counter-cultural of modernity, and refuses to be involved in the capitalist mainstream. This will be explored further in Chapter 7.

The term creates problems when used in the field. Indeed, as Lewis realises:

> For anyone researching the New Age movement, the reflections found in "Is 'New Age' Dead?" raise several important issues. In the first place, because individuals, institutions, and periodicals who formerly referred to themselves as "New Age" no longer identify themselves as such, studies built around a distinction between New Age and non-New-Age become more complex. (Lewis in Lewis *et al.* 1992: 2)

Further, this term also lacks a clear denotation in the academic literature and among the likes of the New Age spokespersons listed by York (1995: 48-88)[4], such as MacLaine and Gayce.

While it could be argued that the term "New Age" is dead, this popular and often misused word seems very much alive. Another problem is that this term is very often used as a metonymy; that is, as the single descriptor for a range of distinguishable religious phenomena of which it is only a part. York (1995), on the other hand, separates neo-paganism from New Age. In Possamai (1999b), it was found necessary to distinguish three subtypes of these contemporary spiritualities: Aquarian perennism (a modern movement valorising the future and progress), neo-paganism (an anti-modern movement valorising traditions, mainly pagan) and presentist perennism – a movement which has its genesis in postmodernity. These sub-types cannot usefully be conflated under the term New Age. More specifically, these subtypes have a different genesis. The Theosophical Society – an esoteric group from the nineteenth century – has engendered Aquarian perennism, while occultism – another esoteric group from the nineteenth century – has inspired neo-paganism. These two groups were formed in the 1930s and 1940s. Presentist perennism is not connected to a specific esoteric movement but, I argue, has grown out of a cultural shift in industrial societies. Post-industrial societies – including their counter-culture movements – are defined partly in terms of deep cultural changes occurring within them; these include declining belief in the idea of progress, radical individualism, and fluidity of movement between sub-cultures. Presentist perennism, even though it borrows eclectively from earlier esotericism, is to be understood as an expression, in the field of spirituality, of emergent post-industrial or postmodern culture.

---

[4] York (1995) has analysed the spokespersons of NAS in a descriptive way and discusses the fact that some of these people tend to eschew the designation "New Age" (*o.c.*: 49). It is not my intention to summarise the works by Ram Dass, Edgar Gayce, Ruth Montgomery, Shirley MacLaine, etc; for such an analysis, see York (1995).

"Perennism" is a term which attempts to respect the local reality of the participants I interviewed and which is used as a heuristic tool to describe Alternative Spiritualities, a term used in preference to the hermeneutically deficient term "New Age" (Possamai, 2001b). Perennism has three characteristics and is defined as a syncretic spirituality, which interprets the world as *monistic* (the cosmos is perceived as having its elements deeply interrelated. It recognises a single ultimate principle, being, or force, underlying all reality, and rejects the notion of dualism, e.g. mind/body); whose actors are attempting to develop their *Human Potential Ethic* (actors work on themselves for personal growth); and whose actors are seeking *Spiritual Knowledge* (the way to develop oneself is through a pursuit of knowledge, be it the knowledge of the universe or of the self, the two being sometimes interrelated.

The following sections analyse the cultural consumption by perennists – that is, practitioners of perennism or people involved in Alternative Spiritualities – of indigenous culture, history at large (this chapter), and popular culture (next chapter). By cultural consumption, I refer to practices of selectively borrowing, or even shopping for, cultural content in indigenous culture, in history, and in popular culture.

Cultural Appropriation of Indigenous Culture

According to Mick Dodson (1994), the Aboriginal and Torres Strait Islander Social Justice Commissioner of the early 1990s, indigenous people are often romanticised and "exoticised". As he describes in more detail:

> Indigenous people are used to create a counterpoint against which the dominant society can critique itself, becoming living embodiments of the romantic ideal, which offers a desolate society the hope of redemption and of recapturing what it feels it has lost in its march forward. Those who wish to present a critique of individualism point out that Aboriginality is about community; those who wish to highlight the detrimental effects of industrialisation on the environment point to Indigenous people as the original conservationists. We present a remaining, though strategically distant, image of what has been lost, and what could be regained.

More specifically to this chapter, perennists seem to show an interest in indigenous culture, and this creates further problems. According to anthropologist Diane Bell (in Richards, 1995: 61):

> [...] we're talking about highly problematic renditions of beliefs and life ways and people, spiritual selves being put into books, being put onto tapes, being put onto videos, sold across the counter to hungry, desperate people who have very little understanding of what's really going on and in many ways don't want to know. [...] It is insidious and dangerous.

Further, some commentators[5] underscore the power relation in "cultural appropriation" – that is, the processes by which meanings are transformed within specific hierarchical structures of power, and in this case within the structures of race (Marcus, 1998) – and see in "New Age" a quest for cultural inclusiveness that erases all difference and that often reduces indigenous practices to shallow therapeutic devices. For these authors, this quest "invades" the space of Aboriginal people, is neo-colonialist and is a romantic "expropriation" of Aboriginal culture that avoids and even undermines issues such as land rights and self-determination. The claim that these perennists can be like "indigenes" appears to be an attempt to appropriate an identity which is now a source of power

In my fieldwork, I discussed indigenous culture with several informants. Susie was very interested in Aboriginal spirituality and she wanted to learn more from it:

> Feeling like this whole country [Australia] has kind of been abused a lot and that both on a practical and on a spiritual level you have to bring some of its traditional culture back.

Another participant, Elizabeth, thinks it is questionable to appropriate and commodify indigenous culture. Both desire to learn about indigenous spirituality, but only from indigenous people. On the other hand, Lynne Hume (2000) discovered that "it is not only Westerners who are making connections between the 'New Age' and Aboriginal worldviews [but some] individual Aborigines are [also] offering New Age-style workshops of self-discovery, using New Age rhetoric and practices".[6]

There seems to be two "oversimplified" points of view. On one side, (some) indigenous people and (some) social commentators challenge the "expropriation/merchandisation" of indigenous culture. However well intended, the appropriation of indigenous culture appears to be a form of cultural genocide – destroying such traditions. On the other side, it seems that (some) perennists "appropriate" indigenous culture, but on a self-perceived peaceful and respectful level. Those subscribing to the former position appear to attend to the production and distribution of these "expropriations" – i.e. selling of merchandises – and not their reception by (some) people – i.e. the consumption of these merchandises. It could thus be argued that it is reductionist to analyse the "perennist production" of indigenous culture, first, thinking that social actors

---

[5] Such as Denise Cuthbert and Michele Grossman (1996), Julie Marcus (1996; 1998) and the American Indian Movement (AIM) (James Lewis, in Miller (ed.), 1995: 384).

[6] An argument also followed by Pecotic (2001).

receive the message passively, and, second, believing that the interested public becomes similar to the message it receives. For example, the American author Marlo Morgan and her best-selling book, *Mutant Message Down Under* was viewed as exploiting Aboriginal culture for personal profit by some indigenous people and academics, but this book does not necessarily represent the many eclectic views of the New Age Community.[7] Inspired by De Certeau (1988) and by my fieldwork, the perennist commodified version of indigenous culture is not received passively, but is contested and again reappropriated. Because of this, perennists seem to resist the production of indigenous "merchandise" aiming toward a "cultural appropriation". It is for this reason that (some) perennist actors work towards an ethics of appropriation which – it is hoped – will not pose a threat to indigenous cultural integrity and sur-vival, and which will challenge "unintended" forms of racism (see for example Gallagher, 2000; Taylor, 1997).

Recent researches show a paradoxical effect of this Australian "ap-propriation". Mulcok (2001a; 2001b; 2003) argues the possibility that there might be a greater interest in Aboriginal spirituality in European and North American "New Age" milieux – especially in didjeridu music and its "healing powers" (Neuenfeldt, 1998; Welch, 2002) – than in Australia where the interest in indigenous North American spirituality has been more transparent. Mulcock's (2001a) claim is that as a practice in New Age spirituality, many forms of identity are borrowed – or consumed – by the New Age self, but that for unclear reasons, indige-nous North American identities appear to be "consumed" more than the Australian Aboriginal ones by "white Australians".

In this consumer culture that seems to reflect our globalised world, these actors consume indigenous culture, but also history and popular culture. This global "cultural consumption", which could be defined as processes by which meanings are transformed within the self, leads to the "spiritual and the commercial becom[ing] increasingly wedded" (York, 2001a: 372).

However, as I argue in the next section, cultural consumption of in-digenous culture is part of a larger trend, that of cultural consumption of history at large. In this chapter, I do not mean to undermine the prob-lematic involved with the production and consumption of indigenous culture, especially the issues of power and inequalities – however it is beyond the scope of this book to explore the postcolonialist positioning on the "spiritual appropriation" of the "Other", and to explore issues of

---

[7]   See Mulcock (2001b) to understand the difficulty of conducting fieldwork within this field of research.

other "appropriations" such as those via museums and ethnology. It is nevertheless my intention to step back and analyse the bigger picture of perennist practices and focus on the social practice of these consuming actors.

Cultural Consumption of History

Academics are aware of gaps in archaeological evidence, the unreliability of some historical sources, and the limits as to what can safely be inferred from the available data. While it could be argued that non-academic perennists disrespect, even romanticise, history, it does not have the same meaning for them. As one perennist said, "[i]t doesn't matter about strict historicity – it sets up a wonderful warm glow of hope. It helps you feel more integrated" (Bowman, 1993: 152). And as found in a notice in a Celtic shop, "[t]he words and images you see in this room are not about academic accuracy, clever deduction of historic fact. They are language of the heart that speaks to the heart" (*o.c.:* 153). Furthermore, a neo-pagan (in Harrow, 1994) states that "history is, for us, only a source of inspiration to be selectively drawn on".[8] In my fieldwork, I talked to Nicholas and his comment correlates with the non-interest in historical facts described above:

> I believe in symbols. I believe in metaphors. Metaphors and metaphysics is what I believe in. I don't believe in facts. I don't believe in history. I don't believe in those things.

The perennist reappropriation of the past is not objective historicism, but subjective interpretation and sometimes invention of something about which they know little can be said or proved but which feels right. Perennist research in history is not universal historicism but an atomisation – or subjectivisation – of history. In Luhrmann's (1994: 252-253) book on magic in contemporary England, magicians borrow symbols – different images, myths and stories – in a way that is relevant to their lives; and history can also become a symbol and be subjectively reinterpreted.

Could this be interpreted as a non-academic deconstruction of history in which the almost free interpretation of the historian supports some novel understanding (Himmelfarb, 1989: 667)? Perennists seems to subjectively reconstruct history into myths, which may be presented as "poetic" truths; that is, truths which are not presented as "exact" truths and are nevertheless available to those who want to believe in them (see

---

[8]   York (1999) argues that the whole pagan movement, in the West, possesses fictional origins.

Luhrmann, 1994: 259-265). In these myths, there is no satisfactory scientific accuracy. Rather, they make sense to the alogical – magical, intuitive – thinking of perennists. In her research on the meanings of the past for spiritual actors in Brittany, Ellen Bodone (1991: 536) argues for this kind of appropriation of history as a legitimating myth:

> Yet since cultural forms are always socially constituted and reinterpreted in light of historical and contingent concerns, all traditions are, at some level, "invented".

However, if all traditions are "invented", as is the case in perennism, they are nevertheless expressed in a social context. For example, in the nineteenth century, H.P. Blavatsky – the founder of the Theosophical Society –, inspired by Darwinism, was convinced that a subhuman type existed. She believed that "the Australian and African aboriginals are 'narrow-brained' left-overs, far inferior by nature to the 'Aryans' who spearhead mankind's evolutionary course" (Roszak, 1976: 123). This, of course, differs from today's trend valorising indigenous culture as explained in the previous section.

Perennists appear to select what suits them in history for their ethos. This could be explained as an intellectual bricolage *à la carte* used for history. By this, I refer to the notion of individuation of decisions presented by Dobbelaere and Voyé (1990: S4-S6) in which people no longer accept a religious "set menu" offered by "traditional religions" but are more interested in a religion *à la carte*. Describing these independent religious individualists, Dobbelaere and Voyé argue that "the adage, 'I think and I choose my beliefs and practices to express my religious feelings' [has] a tremendous appeal for them". Upon this line of thinking, but more in relation to alternative spiritualities, Hanegraaff (1999) refers to an eclectic private symbolism in which new religious/spiritual syntheses are continually created via an individual manipulation of existing symbolic systems.

This new symbolism also finds inspiration in popular culture where the consumption for signs seems freer. This is explored in the next chapter.

CHAPTER 3

Subjective Myths

Introduction

Judy Horacek is an Australian cartoonist who publishes in the *Australian Magazine* and numerous other places. She has as a theme of predilection postmodernism, poststructuralism, feminism, career advice and how to deal with sticky yellow bits of paper. In one cartoon, we are exposed to a satire of postmodernism. Adam and Eve are told by God to "Go forth & be postmodern" and are expelled from Paradigm. In this play on words – that is, being expelled from Paradigm/Paradise and having to be postmodern/multiple –, we could imagine that paradise is one clear paradigm whereas outside of "paradigm", in the mortal world, living conditions are quite harsh as there are so many multiple narratives – in Lyotard's sense of the word. As Adam and Eve are on earth to multiply, being postmodern is to create as many narratives as possible, as if each human being should have his or her own paradigm, or have, as it will be argued in this chapter in regards to religious consumers, his or her own subjective myth; that is, myths that have relevance to the self.

This chapter explores the cultural consumption of some forms of popular culture as found in various spiritual groups and on the Internet. As discovered in Chapter 2, the term cultural consumption is to be understood as a process by which meanings are transformed within the self. By exploring the works of the French social philosopher, Lipovetsky, this chapter argues that popular culture is freely available for anyone to consume for religious purposes and that this process is part of the spirit of our time.

Consumption of Popular Culture

For the purpose of the following chapters, perennists are to be understood as technical spiritual actors/consumers who find inspiration from popular culture and from an array of diverse religions for the source of their spirituality. The level of inspiration varies from one person to another and it is not the point of this chapter to quantify this spectrum.

The purpose of this chapter is to demonstrate an ideal-type process used extensively by some religious groups, social actors and, to a lesser extent, by some more mainstream individuals. The groups and individuals who make extensive use of popular culture tend to be found in the large family of New Age spiritualities, neo-paganism and new religious movements. However, not all groups from this very extended family follow this process of consumption.

Before theorising this process, the following examples will illustrate how some science fiction, horror, and fantasy narratives can be understood as cultural reservoirs for the construction of religion by spiritual consumers. These cultural reservoirs are used as a base for a faith which in turn is consumed by the individual.

The Church of All Worlds is a neo-pagan group founded in 1962 in the USA. It was founded by Oberon Zell in Missouri and moved to Ukiah, California, in 1967. It was formed in Australia in 1992 by Fiona and Anthorr Nomchong and became the first recognised Goddess and Earth Worshiping religion within this country. This group bases its teaching in part on Robert Heinlein's *Stranger in a Strange Land* which narrates the story of Valentine Michael Smith – a Martian living on earth with god-like powers who taught humankind how to love. The group is not limited to the reading of this novel and even extends its consumption to the *Star Trek* mythos; as one of their members states:

> This whole period (late 1960s) fell under the shadow of the Damoclean Sword of impending nuclear holocaust, and a dominant Christian culture that fully embraced an apocalyptic mythos. For many of us, a powerful antidote to that mythos was found in science fiction, and particularly Gene Roddenberry's *Star Trek*, with its Vulcan IDIC: "Infinite Diversity in Infinite Combinations". CAW [Church of All Worlds] and Green Egg avidly embraced this vision of, as Roddenberry said, "a future everyone will want to be part of".[1]

Another movement clearly inspired by science fiction, and more specifically by Ron Hubbard's stories, is the Church of Scientology, which is sometimes referred to as the "Science Fiction Religion" (Cohen *et al.*, 1987: 331). During the 1940s, science fiction was beginning to explore themes concerning the powers of the mind, and John W. Cambell encouraged such stories in the leading US magazine *Astounding Science Fiction*. The founder of the Church, Hubbard, who was at that time a science fiction and adventure writer, published an article which formed the basis of his religion in the May 1950 issue of *Astounding Science Fiction*, titled "Dianetics: The Evolution of Science". Although this

---

[1]   Internet site, http://www.greenegg.org/issues/123/oberonedit123.html (05/01/00).

article and a book published at the same time, *Dianetics: The Modern Science of Mental Health*, caused a sensation, many science fiction fans and writers claimed that the creation of the religion has no connection at all with science fiction (Holdstock, 1978: 197).

The *Star Wars* mythos is also idiosyncratically borrowed by individuals to support their spirituality. There is an Internet site which gives a detailed religious/spiritual explanation of the force entitled: "A Way to the Force by Yoda of Dabobah"[2] which is based on meditation techniques. In Australia, "The *Star Wars* Appreciation Society" has attempted to establish Jedi as an officially recognised religion and has even ambushed the 2001 national census (Duff, 2001). More will follow on *Star Wars* in the following chapters.

Other science-fiction narratives opened, or even popularised, the doors of extraordinary perception and appeal to these spiritual consumers: e.g. the *Star Trek* series – which is a source of inspiration for some neo-pagan groups (Hume, 1997: 55) –, *E.T.* (Rushing, 1985), the *X-Files* and *Buffy the Vampire Slayer* (Introvigne, 2001a). *2001, A Space Odyssey* is for Williams (1984), essentially a "religious" film and has, according to DeMet (2001), been described by many viewers as a religious experience. Indeed, it can be argued that in the last sequence of the movie, Stanley Kubrick (the director) stirs emotions, subconscious and a mythological yearning in the viewer (Agel, 1970: 161). In less than five minutes, the hero ages quickly and then is reborn as a baby floating in the stars. Further, the newborn who floats among celestial bodies, the star-child, not only reveals a new humankind of a high mental and spiritual development, but the music by Richard Strauss also denotes the coming of a new knowledge that will be shared – the descent of the mountain by Zarathustra.

One should not forget the Heaven's Gate group that committed a mass suicide in San Diego in 1997. Its members believed that a UFO was travelling behind the Hale-Bop comet and that by leaving their physical bodies behind, they would reach the extraterrestrial realm. They also watched the *X-Files* and *Star Trek* almost religiously and took fiction seriously. Indeed, as one member expressed a week before the infamous event:

> We watch a lot of *Star Trek*, a lot of *Star Wars*, it's just, to us, it's just like going on a holodeck. We've been training on a holodeck [... and] now it's time to stop. The game's over. It's time to put into practice what we've learned. We take off the virtual reality helmet [...] go back out of the

---

2   Internet site, http://www.quantumlight.com/theforce/writings/force/the_force.htm (03/02/00).

holodeck to reality to be with, you know, the other members on the craft in the heavens. (quoted by Robinson, 1997)

As Robinson (1997) comments, these members have envisioned death as the ultimate Trekkie trip to the final frontier.

Horror stories can also provide a reservoir of cultural content to be consumed. In 1966, in San Francisco, Anton LaVey founded the Church of Satan as a medium for the study of the Black Arts. His assumption of the inherent selfishness and violence of human beings is at the base of its non-Christian teaching. Satan, the mistaken long time opponent of God, according to LaVey, is a hidden force in nature that can be tapped into. In *The Satanic Rituals* – which is used by some as a basis for metaphysical growth –, LaVey (1972) refers to the metaphysics of H.P. Lovecraft, the writer of weird fiction who wrote most of his tales during the 1920s and 1930s. H.P. Lovecraft developed a pantheon of gods, the Ancient Ones – e.g. Cthulhu, Yog-Sothoth and Nyarlathotep –, who are waiting in secrecy before coming back to earth to conquer the human race. In *The Nameless City* (1921), Lovecraft introduced the mad Arab Abdul Alhazred who had penned the ancient tome *The Necronomicon*. This book, claiming to reveal all secrets of the world, especially those of the Ancient Ones, became a standard prop in all later stories, and many readers believed it actually existed. Lovecraft always claimed that his stories were fictional and that he was a total agnostic. However, LaVey (1972), believing that "fantasy plays an important part in any religious curriculum", developed some rituals for his Church of Satan based on this fictional mythology. The following is a ceremony extract:

N'kgnath ki'q Az-Athoth r'jyarh wh'fagh zhasa phr-tga nyena phragn'glu.

Translation: Let us do honor to Azathoth, without whose laughter this world should not be.

The influence of Lovecraft is also found in the more recent phenomenon of Teenage Satanism (Lowney, 1995) and felt in other groups such as the Esoteric Order of Dagon and the Order of the Trapezoid[3], from the Temple of Set[4], which is a chivalric order of knighthood.

Exploring different types of Orders, we can find that groups such as The Temple of the Vampire[5] and the Order of the Vampyre[6] base their religiosity on vampire fictions. And as the Order states on its Internet site: "We are not looking at the blood-sucking gore that has made

---

[3] Internet site, http://www.trapezoid.org/statement.html (18/04/00).
[4] Internet site, http://www.xeper.org/pub/tos/noframe.htm (18/04/00).
[5] Internet site, http://home.netcom.com/~temple/vampire/html (18/04/00).
[6] Internet site, http://www.xeper.org/pub/tos/orders/VAM-ST.htm (18/04/00).

Dracula and others like him the archetypical Vampyres of legend. But we are looking at some of the alleged powers of the creature, such as invisibility and manipulation". Even if some members ritually suck blood from each other "from a finger pierced", their practice is only metaphorical vampirism (Introvigne, 1997).

Today, a visit to the "Gothic" and "Vampyres" Internet sites reveals large numbers wanting to become vampires and gain superpowers. Some gothic witches have even a strong affinity with vampires (Hume, 1997: 55). Even if the vampire has been popular since the nineteenth century, "it has never had as pervasive an appeal in American popular culture as it has had in the past decade" (Schopp, 1997: 232). For Auerbach (1995: 155), the character of the vampire was revised in the 1970s arousing a longing for personal transformation. During this period, vampires were "more frightened than frightening" and became "at their worst, edifying, Superman-like rescuers"[7]. The vampire can be attractive to fans because of its embodiment of power, and can be a source of inspiration for spiritual consumers.

Moving away from the vampire but staying around the same genre, Keyworth (2004) opens our eyes on a werewolf – or lycanthrope – subculture in which individuals follow particular traditions such as that of the Vicking berserkers, that of the South American jaguar cults or that of the native American tradition involving coyotes. By various means, such as "mental" shifting in which the practitioner involves the animalistic nature and acquires some paranormal power – as claimed to be practiced by the Vickings of the medieval period – the individual is said to enhance his or her physical abilities and senses. There would be few groups who provide mutual support and guidance for fellow werewolfs and new comers on the Internet.

More specifically to neo-paganism, the literature labelled "Fantasy" seems to express and explore neo-pagan issues (Harvey 2000; Luhrmann 1994). J.R.R. Tolkien's *Lord of the Rings*, Marion Bradley's *The Mist of Avalon*, Brian Bates's *The Way of Wyrd*, Terry Pratchett's *Discworld* corpus, and even Gibson's cyber-punk *Neuromancer* and Wagner's operas, are all parts of a cultural reservoir which contribute to neo-pagan thinking. While there is no "biblical" text of reference in neo-paganism, the construction of the pagan self entails reading works of

---

[7] The author analyses the different perception of the vampire and discovers that before Bram Stoker's novel, narrators of vampire's stories – especially Byron – were not repelled by this being, on the contrary, there was hope of becoming equally uncommon. Between Stoker's *Dracula* and the 1970s, vampires were imprisoned in their transformation and did not offer an exaltation of their transfiguring power.

fiction. These fantasy books describe a pagan world and consequently contribute to the pagan experience of the reader (Harvey, 2000).

In Ellwood (2004), we discover how some people involved in the craft use popular culture as a method of practicing magic. In this text, the author explains how he uses the character of Buffy the Vampire Slayer as a god-form of protection, equality, and magic. Instead of using magic and incantation in the name of one god as often practised in religions comprising a large pantheon of gods, certain neo-pagans use icons of popular culture instead of more traditional gods. The importance behind these magical practices/rituals is to focus one's energy on the characteristic of this god/pop icon. For example, as the author (*o.c.*: 187) explains:

> Let me give you a quick example. You may want to go on a diet, but know under ordinary circumstances you'd have trouble keeping to it. You can use the magick of working with a pop culture entity to help you. Who do you use? Were I to go on a diet I'd use the pop culture entity Jared, who represents the Subway franchise. You'll see him a lot on US television and each time he's showing the benefits of a successful diet. So what you do is create a god-form out of Jared. Observe the commercials, take notes on attributes you'd want your Jared god-form to have and then on the first night of the diet and each night after invoke the Jared god-form to help you keep to the diet. Now on a humorous aside you may find yourself having an inexplicable craving for Subway subs, but so be it. As long as you are dieting and reaching your target weight it doesn't matter. What does matter is that you invest Jared with your belief that he will keep you dieting. Use chants, images, and whatever else as needed.

The need for a pop icon, according to this testimony should only be for the time that one person needs it. After this, the practitioner should move to another pop icon. The danger if this is not acted upon, is that one person might start believing too much in this icon, instead of using it for a specific purpose.

Theodore Roszak (1976: 23-24) finds in science fiction, sword-and-sorcery, and I should add, horror fictions, an array of "romances enjoying an almost reverential respect as doors of extraordinary perception". They all depict heroes and/or anti-heroes meeting supernatural characters or travelling in fantasy worlds, or, at an extreme, changing into supernatural creatures. Truzzi (1972) notes increasing comfort with the paranormal in popular culture, such as the phenomenon of teenagers spending the night in supposedly haunted houses. Truzzi reflected on the character of the witch, which if once negatively stigmatised, is now viewed as glamorous amongst the middle-class youth. "Glamorous" horror literature also invades children's literature. Monsters and ghosts are no longer exclusively described to scare but also to entertain the young readers. These fictions have, it appears, some of its "supernatural entities" tamed, and thus offer a reservoir of cultural themes to be consumed.

In a more mainstream narrative genre, *The Celestine Prophecy* – a novel describing the quest or path of the development of the inner self of the hero – is a source of inspiration for many people. The author of this novel, James Redfield (1994), now has an Internet site which promotes his new spirituality:

> Our belief is that there is a growing worldwide interest in spirituality that is creating a new spiritual awareness and culture that will flourish in the new millennium. Yet we realize that no one person has the ultimate perspective and so, this Celestine WebSite is dedicated to an ongoing spiritual discussion and the dissemination of ideas throughout the world.[8]

There are also other groups, independent of Redfield, which use the *Celestine Prophecy* as a metaphor for their spirituality: such as the New Civilization Network, described as a "global network of people visualising a better world and working on building it. A world of increased quality of life, freedom, fun and inspiration for all. A world where the needs of all of humanity are met."[9] The group started on March 13th, 1995 from an informal e-mail message in a Internet discussion group which created a significant amount of feedback and interest in working with such a site.

There are also Internet sites developed by individuals which are mainly used as "vehicles for introducing themselves to the world, featuring photographs and biographies that contribute to a careful construction of the self" (Smith, 1999: 88). Some of them present their idiosyncratic view on spiritualities. These sites have some links with other sites about spirituality or about work of fictions supporting their view of life. Two examples of this type of site are *Quavajo*[10] and *New Age Insights on Spiritual Growth and Expanded Consciousness*[11] which promote the diffusion of people's personal spiritual journey and help to deepen people's understanding of their "true self".

Arguably, popular culture – and some Internet sites – offers a library of myths or narratives to be consumed and idiosyncratically reconstructed into subjective myths – as I will argue soon – by its readers. However, before exploring what is meant by subjective myths, an

---

[8]   Internet site, www.celestinevision.com (28/01/00).
[9]   Internet site, http://www.newciv.org/ncn/ncnintro.html (28/01/00).
[10] Internet site, http://www.geocities.com/Athens/Delphi/ 2911/ (3/02/00).
[11] Internet site, http://home.earthlink.net/~den_is/ (3/02/00).

understanding of Lipovetsky's work on the spirit of our time will help us to contextualise this phenomenon.

Cultural Consumption, Lipovetsky, and the Postmodern Individual

Detailing people's taste of culture in a postmodern society in which signs and symbols are innovated at a rapid flow, especially when many of these spiritual consumers are not strictly confined to religious communities or churches, but are dispersed through many networks (Possamai, 2000b), leads to difficulty when trying to understand major trends in their cultural consumption. There are neither ecclesiastics nor demarcated doxies and rituals, and these practitioners are more interested in experience than in doctrine, and belief systems are often amalgams of disparate doctrines based on understanding realised through experience. Their shared view includes thinking mainly by affinity and refusing conventional systematic deductive logic.

Another overlapping problem is the extreme individualism of these perennists. In their discourse, they offer indeterminacy rather than determinism, diversity rather than unity, difference rather than synthesis, complexity rather than simplification. As one of my respondents declared:

> The labels that we [perennists] use tend to be unfortunately widespread and because they're being used by so many people they have many different resonances in people's minds.

The different discourses of these actors read like a postmodern intertextuality in which the reader wanders in imagination and interpretations, and this makes the task of understanding this cultural consumption at a more macro level than that of the individual problematic.

Despite this difficulty, it is possible to understand this cultural consumption through the work of Featherstone (1991). He identifies three types of theories of consumer culture. The first analyses consumerism as a stage of capitalist development. The second is a more sociological concern about how people delineate their class and status and how they create distinction via their consuming habits. The third is concerned with the creativity of consumer practices and how this leads to an aesthetics and emotional pleasure of consumption.[12] Because of the creativity involved in this process of consumption, this section will concentrate on the third theory using the works of Lipovetsky (1987; 1993). Follow-

---

[12] The first and third theories have already been explored in the previous chapter.

ing this postmodern approach, the consumer's identity is viewed as undergoing a process of unceasing construction.

For Lipovetsky (1987; 1993), consumption is about the construction of individual identity. The French author gives an analysis of advanced "modern" societies, and argues that if roles, norms, and class were at the focus of the older social world, we now live in a social world in which life is organised around the individual as consumer. In this world, the individual is autonomous, seeks his or her potential, constructs who he or she is, and is part of the great adventure of the self.

Lipovetsky (1993) refers to a second revolution of individualism that occurred in postmodernity[13] which is characterised by narcissism. In this revolution, the knowledge of oneself is central (*ca*.: 91). Those caught up in these changes mainly focus their attention on themselves and do not invest in "macro identities" such as class, gender, ethnicity, and religion as much as in the past. They focus on constructing their own identity, their own personality, and on generating their own "narcissistic" knowledge. Indeed, in today's times, it is no longer important to be of the same class, religious background and education to that of our parents. If before we inherited our social characteristics from our family and kept them as part of our identity for the rest of our life, today, it can be argued that we make ourselves who we want to be. For example, in the sphere of religion, we can even explore different religions and pick-and-mix various parts electively and make it a personal spirituality. As an illustration, in Australia, it is now less important to be an Irish Catholic like our parents. We can still remain Catholic, but we can also explore and choose *à la carte* other religious elements to create a personal identity and spirituality; or move away from Catholicism and still consume *à la carte*, such as studying astrology, being interested in Tibetan Buddhism, re-reading the Bible and re-watching the *Star Wars* saga, etc. This activity is more a lifestyle than a way of life[14]. Chaney (1996) describes the sensibilities employed by the social actor in consuming and in articulating these cultural resources as mode of personal expression. In this sense, we could speak about a postmodern religious lifestyle when dealing with these bricoleurs.

These new forms of sociability enrich the realm of private activity and pleasures, and consist of the ramification of modes of individual

---

[13] For Lipovetsky, the first revolution of individualism happened with modernity, but this individualism was mainly restricted to the economic sphere and to some *avant-garde* movements.

[14] A way of life tends to be typically associated with a more-or-less stable community.

consumption; indeed, leisure-time is extended and resources are mainly devoted to private consumption and pastimes, including religion.

It is tempting, indeed, to bring the quest to understand this cultural consumption to a close by concluding that this consumption is essentially and exclusively individualistic; that there is nothing shared except the exaltation of individual eclecticism. Lipovetsky (1987) would describe this as a frivolous economy; that is, consumers set their own goals and design their own lives guided only by hedonistic values. These consumers eschew available macro-identities. They are mobile and their tastes fluctuate.

Postmodernity has been defined not only in terms of cultural traits, as described above, but in terms of a broad personality profile. Roseneau (1992: 53-54) describes the postmodern individual – an ideal-type portrait – as such:

> The post-modern individual is relaxed and flexible, oriented toward feelings and emotions, interiorization, and holding a "be-yourself" attitude. S/he is an active human being constituting his/her own social reality, pursuing a personal quest for meaning but making no truth claims for what results.

We can understand from this description that these spiritual consumers seek their personal quest for meaning by consuming diverse parts of religions and popular culture. However, the description of this postmodern individual continues:

> S/he looks to fantasy, humour, the culture of desire, and immediate gratification. Preferring the temporary over the permanent, s/he is contented with a "live and let live" (in the present) attitude. More comfortable with the spontaneous that the planned, the post-modern individual is also fascinated with tradition, the antiquated (the past in general), the exotic, the sacred, the unusual, and the place of the local rather than the general or the universal.

As already seen in the previous chapter, since this consumer society is not restricted to "material" commodities but to culture as well – which is the very element of consumer society itself (Featherstone, 1991: 85) – texts are consumed by the reader, construct who the reader is, and (re)define the reader's self in his or her involvement in this culture of desire. If malls are crowded with shoppers who construct their sense of self through buying commodities, in the case of this analysis, these spiritual consumers construct their sense of self through consuming popular culture. As seen previously, consumption is not limited to popular culture but is extended to other religions, to history and to indigenous culture(s).

Finding a rationale behind this consumption seems to be problematic. Indeed, from this "postmodern" perspective, the individual consumer is not necessarily a coherent subjectivity searching for particular rewards, but a more open-ended form of identity that is neither intrinsically rational or consistent. (Chaney 1996, 76)

Subjective Myths and Meta-Consumption

We have just observed various consumptions of popular culture, and the theory laid down by Lipovetsky helps us to contextualise this phenomenon which appears to be part of the spirit of the time for certain strata of the Western world.

In this case, as seen in this and the previous chapter, these consumers not only select their religion/spirituality and popular culture *à la carte* (Possamai, 2000a) as a main meal, but they also select parts of history as an *entrée*. This subjective "tasteful meal" of religion/spirituality and history is digested into an even more subjective myth. Indeed,

> Traditionally, "mythology" has been viewed as a body of stories aimed at explaining the human condition, which is well-known to a particular culture or society. However, in a contemporary context, "mythology" can be said to involve stories or imagery known primarily to the self. Just as people feel free to pick and choose from various world religious traditions, they also feel relatively free to create a highly personalized mythos that has explanatory power only in regard to the self. (Bloch, 1998: 99)

In this sense, myths can be understood as a set of images known primarily to the self. And as these consumers freely choose their religions/spiritualities and interpret/select parts of history, as they culturally consume religion(s), history, and popular culture, they create their subjective mythology which "has explanatory power only in regard to the self".

There are, of course, different levels of mythological subjectivism. Some spiritual consumers do not belong to any group and consume popular culture and create their own personal subjective myths. However, some of these consumers can belong to a group such as the Church of All Worlds and the Church of Satan described above. Within some of these groups, members might share the group's "official" subjective myth, or might share some elements of it only. Further, some of the subjective myths created from this consuming process by certain practitioners can also be consumed by other spiritual consumers; this process being called the meta-consumption of subjective myths. To illustrate this "avid" consumption, we shall now turn to a shared and multi-constructed "subjective myth" found in New Age at large; that of the Age of Aquarius.

Astrology has many branches and schools with a wide variety of astrological theories. One of them – which deals with nations and people –

is called religious astrology, as set out by Le Cour (1995). Just as a chart can be drawn for an individual, so too for a society. Following Le Cour, some modern astrologers claim that the sun changes its zodiacal sign every 2160 years, according to the astrological law of the precession of equinoxes. This migration into another zodiac is supposed to create important modifications on earth; and just such a profound alteration is about to happen in the third millennium. The sun is leaving the zodiac of Pisces and will gradually enter the zodiac of Aquarius, affecting the behaviour and attitudes of every living creature. This is referred to as the coming of the Age of Aquarius.

Based on this interpretation of the scripture of the stars, some astrologers consume selective parts of history and reconstruct it into an astrological narration. The following is a summary account.

In the ninth and tenth centuries BC, the world was passing through the Age of Leo, the ruler of the sun. For these astrologers, this Age was therefore marked by sun worshipping. Then followed the Age of Cancer, a water sign that was seen to be the cause of the Great Flood. Because Cancer is ruled by the moon, this Age was also characterised by moon cults and worship of female divinities. The Age of Gemini, 6000 to 4000 BC, saw the invention of writing, because Gemini's ruler, Mercury, is the planet of communication. The Age of Taurus brought the worship of the bull, of the Golden Calf and also the construction of pyramids, ziggurats and other important constructions because Taurus is, in astrology, the fixed Earth sign. The Age of Aries brought ram worship. During this period, Abram changed his name to Abraham - which means "coming from the ram" or "son of the ram". Then came the Age of Pisces and the consequence of its appearance was the growth of Christianity. The fish became a secret sign by which early Christians recognised one another in the midst of hostile nonbelievers.

Because of the sun's appearance during the vernal equinox in the zodiac of Aquarius, humankind will be influenced in attitude and behaviour under the Aquarian "totem". Aquarians, in astrology's own positive interpretation, are brilliant and inventive and also persistent and determined. They are also greatly concerned to help others. It is therefore deduced from this identity that the paradigmatic characteristics of the world in the Aquarian Age will be orderliness, constructiveness and intelligence.

This Aquarian eschatology, however, is not followed by all New Agers (Possamai, 1999b). Several of my informants were anxious to dissociate themselves from Aquarian history. Sarah is one of them and finds a certain arrogance in Aquarian history:

Sarah: I think it's arrogant to think that things get better as we go along and progress. We don't progress. It's cyclic [...]. I think we're all heading for another kind of spiritual time. But we could lose it and we probably will. Things seem to be cyclic. You get so far and then you go back and as I said there's nothing we've got that I don't think that people have had before at certain times and in different cultures. Egyptian culture, etc. It may be expressed in different ways, maybe not. I don't know, is there a word for being time centric?

Interviewer: Time centric?

Sarah: Rather than ego centric. Yeah well I think we do. [...] Well you know how you can be ethnocentric and think that your culture's got it the best? [...] Yeah we can suffer from being time centric, but I don't know if there's a word for it.

Steve is disillusioned with some of the myths constructed in his circle. Even if he used to believe in the Age of Aquarius, he never took it as a fact, he only consumed it mythopoetically.

Steve: The new eon, Age of Aquarius, new age are all the same, utopian theme, are going in different names. Yeah definitely. Very strong one in Western occultism is the new age. The dawning of the age of the goddess or the dawning of the age of the new aeon or the Age of Aquarius or the new age, whatever. It's a very important thing in it. Like the end of the Age of Pisces, that stuff, yes. That's a major feature of the whole thing. I think everyone agrees on that one. They just don't agree where and when.

Interviewer: Do you agree that the new age will arrive soon?

Steve: I don't believe any of that crap any more,

Interviewer: Used to?

Steve: I used to use it mythopoetically. I never believed in it factually.

Among Aquarians – that is, New Agers who believe in the Age of Aquarius – there is no consensus on the date of arrival of this Age and on the effect of this shift (see Possamai, 1999a). For some it is necessary to work hard, such as meditating to create a positive flow of energy, so the coming can be more effective. Some of the Aquarian believers expect a Christ of second coming to mark the new era. It can be viewed as a form of energy that will be spread among everyone – or the elect – on earth. For others, this new energy will be embodied in a person, e.g. Maitreya.

From this case study on the Age of Aquarius, it can be thus argued that spiritual consumers not only borrow from popular culture and history to construct their subjective myths but also from already constructed subjective myths; this process is the meta-consumption of subjective myths.

CHAPTER 4

Hyper-Real Religion

Introduction

Fantasy fictions are constructed stories and worlds that mix mythologies from a vast range of ethnic pantheons with scientific and
constructed historical data. Chivalric or medieval romance such as the
Arthurian cycle of legends is the template for classic modern fantasy,
also called at times "sword and sorcery" fiction. For the purpose of this
chapter, I make a difference between fantasy and other-sub genres such
as horror fiction, science fiction, urban fantasy and magic realism.[1] The
fantasy world is not a reconstruction of an imagined past, it is total
construction by the imagination of the author following a set of principles. Indeed, the genre has now so strongly been codified by established
modern authors, such as Tolkien (*The Lord of the Rings*) and Robert E.
Howard (*Conan the Barbarian*), that all contemporary authors must
follow the traditional structure of fantasy worlds and creatures to create
renewed stories. All these stories involve magic, creatures, thieves,
warriors, druids and wizards. They deal with creatures on various quests
meeting the extraordinary in mythic lands. This literature was also a
strong mythic support for the birth of roleplaying games such as *Dungeons & Dragons* which was popular in the 1980s and is seen today as
the classic of them all. This genre has also been successfully adapted to
the giant screen (e.g. the trilogy of *The Lord of the Rings* by Peter
Jackson) and on many computer games (e.g. *Ultima* and *Final Fantasy*).

In 2002, came a new game that changed the code of fantasy. The
game *Kingdom Hearts* is a fantasy game with the usual story lines and
sub-text of a classical fantasy narrative and has the breadth of the usual
characters. It is the story of Sora, a 14-year-old Manga-looking character
carrying a sword shaped like a key, who decides to discover the world
with his two friends, Kairi and Riku. Before the beginning of their
planned quest, they are separated under mysterious conditions and Sora

---

[1] In the literature, fantasy fiction is sometimes used as the encompassing appellation
    that re-groups all of these sub-genres.

finds himself in an unknown town. He starts searching for his two companions and hopes to come back home with them. What makes it different with this fantasy game for young players is that Disney characters have a strong place. The characters of movies such as *Tarzan, Aladdin, Peter Pan, Beauty and the Beast, The 101 Dalmatians, Alice in Wonderland* are all present as if they were part of a classic fantasy world such as elves, orcs, hobbits and dragons.

The fantasy style has a specific set of codes and sub-texts and stories always use as referents classical mythology (e.g. Greek, Roman, Norse, Hindu, Pacific, African, Icelandic, Arabian and British), history (e.g. Antiquity and Middle Ages) and other established fantasy stories (e.g. *Lord of the Rings*), but never before Disney movies. The classical references in this genre are blurred in this computer game and the connection with "traditional" fantasy is obscure. However, the reference to the commodified Disney characters and worlds is clear.[2] Fantasy has never been "real", however with the addition of Disney characters and thus another layer of fiction, the "real" – that is, the "clear" connection with traditional fantasy plots – seems to be greatly broken down; it has become hyper-real.

We have discovered in the last chapters that individuals who consume their spirituality via popular culture – and via history – create their own subjective myths. Further to this analysis, we need to explore another phenomenon not researched yet, but part of the spirit of our time; what I call hyper-real religion. In this religion, the "real" has been broken down and connection with the "real" sources of religion can be blurred. This phenomenon has just been quickly described with the example of *Kingdom Hearts* and this chapter will now focus on a specific case study involving the religious consumption of popular culture; that of the consumption of the *Star Wars* mythos.

The Jedi Religion

We recently received the news: 70,509 people, that is 0.37% of the 2001 Australian population, has identified with the Jedi religion from *Star Wars* (AAP, 2002). Is it a joke or does this reflect a trend that social scientists of religion should seriously take into account? Out of this amount the Australian Star Wars Appreciation Society President estimates that about 5,000 people would be true hard-core people that would believe the Jedi religion – most probably at a metaphorical level.

---

2   This, without any doubt, exposes children and young teenagers to the conspicuous consumption – that is, the competitive display of capacity to spend money on inessentials – connected with the Disney world.

He also estimates that 50,000 fans would have put down Jedi Religion just for fun, and 15,000 people "did it just to give the government a bit of curry" (Agence France-Presse, 2002).[3] In one discussion group, one believer in Jediism claims that "it is important to remember that there is a difference between 'Jedi' on a census form and calling oneself a Jediist [...]".[4]

In the United Kingdom, the 2001 census reveals that 390,000 people have declared to be followers of the Jedi "faith"; that is 0.7% of the UK population. John Pullinger, the Director of reporting and analysis at the Office for National Statistics (ONS) claims that the Jedi supporters are in their late teens and 1920s (Anonymous, 2003).

In my fieldwork, I have met people who use the *Star Wars* mythos to support their religious views of the world. Christina – a so-called New Ager – spoke about a flow of energy that surrounds us, and she made reference to the metaphor of the force from *Star Wars*:

> It's like if I can use a *Star Wars* term, you know. Just went to see *Star Wars* again. It's like you know they keep talking about this force. That's whatever word you want to use. I believe that's there and that's not the physical body but the energy which creates the physical body, and I believe it is there and that somehow it can be tapped into.

Moving towards the Internet medium, we can discover that the introduction to the "Jedi Knight Movement" discussion list states[5]:

> The Way of Jedi transcends the science fiction series of *Star Wars*. It encompasses many of the same truths and realizations of the major world religions, including Zen Buddhism, Taoism, Hinduism, Catholicism, and Shinto and is both a healing art and a meditative journey that the aspirant can take to improve every aspect of their life.

One of the messages from the same "Jedi Knight Movement" discussion list states about "Jediknightism":

> Life on planet earth has become much more complex – the churches, although meaning well, many times fall short of the mark of addressing the complexities. The political arena many times disappoint us and fall short of inspiring either ourselves or others to action.

We can read from this statement that the people who embrace this religion are critical of mainstream religions and of political movements.

---

[3] At the time of the writing of this book, I have not come across data from a more academic source.

[4] Internet site, http://www.jediism.net/forum/viewtopic.php?t=177 (5/08/04).

[5] Internet site, http://groups.yahoo.com/groups/Jedi_Knight_Movement/ (25/10/2002).

Left without these grand narratives, as presented on the site, they are left with another type of narrative:

> Storytelling is an age-old tradition that has followed mankind for millennia – and has been used effectively for transferring ideals, from philosophers to prophets. It is an ideal medium to both entertain and enlighten simultaneously, which is why it is so powerful and its effects so profound when used expertly.

From a glance on this site, it become clear that it entails a desire by interested people to develop their spiritual potential outside of mainstream religions, that they are critical of governments and that they can do this in an entertaining fashion.

On "Jediism: the Jedi Religion"[6], an Internet site dedicated to present Jediism as a religion, we can find that this specific view of the *Star Wars* mythos does not base its focus on the myth and fiction as written by the movie director George Lucas, but upon the "real life" examples of Jediism. As explained:

> Jediism is not the same as that which is portrayed within the Star Wars Saga by George Lucas and Lucasfilm LTD. George Lucas' Jedi are fictional characters that exist within a literary and cinematic universe. The Jedi discussed within this website refer to factual people within this world that live or lived their lives according to Jediism, of which we recognize and work together as a community to both cultivate and celebrate. [...] The history of the path of Jediism traverses through which is well over 5,000 years old. It shares many themes embraced in Hinduism, Confucianism, Buddhism, Gnosticism, Stoicism, Catholicism, Taoism, Shinto, Modern Mysticism, the Way of the Shaolin Monks, the Knight's Code of Chivalry and the Samurai warriors. We recognize that many times the answer to mankind's problems comes from within the purified hearts of genuine seekers of truth. Theology, philosophy and religious doctrine can facilitate this process, but we believe that it would be a futile exercise for any belief system to claim to hold all the answers to all the serious questions posed to seekers of truth in the 21st century. Jediism may help facilitate this process, yet we also acknowledge that it is up to the true believer who applies the universal truths inherent with Jediism to find the answers they seek.

The site then lists different resources on meditation for Jediism such as the Force, the Temple Jedi, and the 7 steps guide – which are seven steps towards effective prayer. Malhotra (2001) in his introductory book on yogic philosophy draws some close similarities between this mythos and his philosophy of meditation.

---

6   Internet site, http://www.jediism.bigstep.com/ (7/03/03).

Moving away from the different consumptions to the production of this mythos, in an interview[7] with George Lucas, the *Star Wars* creator states:

I don't see Star Wars as profoundly religious. I see Star Wars as taking all the issues that religion represents and trying to distil them down into a more modern and easily accessible construct. [...] I put the force into the movie in order to try to awaken a certain kind of spirituality in young people – more a belief in God than a belief in any particular religious system. I wanted to make it so that young people would begin to ask questions about the mystery [...] I didn't want to invent a religion. I wanted to try to explain in a different way the religions that have already existed. I wanted to express it all. [...] I'm telling an old myth in a new way.

Asked about the question if young people seem to be turning to movies for their inspiration instead of organised religion, Lucas' answer is:

Well, I hope that doesn't end up being the course this whole thing takes, because I think there's definitely a place for organized religion. I would hate to find ourselves in a completely secular world where entertainment was passing for some kind of religious experience.

Are we moving towards this phenomenon? Will people use entertainment as a kind of religious experience? We have already noticed in the last chapter that some people follow that process, and I will argue in the last section of this chapter that this tendency might be growing in the near future.

Becoming a Jedi Knight, or working towards such state of being, appears attractive to anyone who wants to develop his or her spiritual abilities. Since Jediknightism, or Jediism, is presented as an old religion re-mythologised to a contemporary public, old techniques of development of the self such as meditation, yoga, and shamanism are used towards this Jedi path. But what is that path?

In Possamai (2000b), I discovered three ideal-types of works towards spiritually developing oneself; that is, what I call the teleologies of the being. The first type is the illuminational development. It is a quest for a direct inner personal experience of the divine within, or for a greater individual potential. This potential includes greater insight, body awareness, and communication with others. It leads to personal growth and development of latent abilities. Spirituality is here an end in itself. The second type is instrumental development. It refers to some techniques an individual uses to better himself or herself, and to become more effective and efficient in worldly pursuits. This teleology leads to wanting to

---

7   Internet site, http://www.next-wave.org/may99/starwars.htm (7/03/03) from an interview with Bill Moyer published in *Time Magazine*, 153 (16), April 26, 1999.

becoming a more "powerful" person in everyday life and focus their attention, not on an inner experience specifically, but on concrete effects, e.g. to develop their intelligence, their charisma, and to feel better in their body. This spiritual development, in this sense, is a means to external ends. The third type of development is entertainment. Some people will work on their spiritual self to develop their higher self (illuminational development) or to gain more power (instrumental development), but others will be involved in some practices just for a good time. In previous research, Luhrmann (1994: 222) argues that people turn to modern magic, "because they seek for powerful emotional and imaginative religious experience, but not for a religion *per se*". Heelas (1993: 111) also refers sarcastically to yuppie (like) people who consume a more Disney-esque – i.e. entertaining – spirituality.

Thus, if a spiritual consumer believes in developing his or her inner spiritual abilities in the hope of developing their spiritual self, he or she will consume certain means in relation to this goal, e.g. use of yoga or Jediism for meditation. If a person fixes a goal in the everyday life to reach a state of well-being, of realisation, he or she will consume other mediums, or he or she consume the same means but with a different conception, e.g. use of yoga or Jediism to diminish stress. Furthermore, a person can be involved in this practice for an entertainment purpose, e.g. use of yoga or Jediism to socialise and have fun. These three types are of course deeply interrelated and many individuals may easily fit with more than one ideal type.

As I will argue in Chapter 5, the mixture of popular culture and religion has created new forms of identification to spiritual consumers, particularly the spread of characters with superpowers such as superheroes in comics, vampires, and Jedi Knights. This might have helped to re-enforce a belief in people to gain (super) abilities in their spiritual and/or everyday life.

This practice of using popular culture for spiritual purpose is not limited to *Star Wars*, as we have already explored with the case of the Church of All World and the Church of Satan in the previous chapter.

It seems that for these spiritual consumers, the real and the unreal might have imploded and might have created an unclear sense of distinction between them. Baudrillard (1988) who has theorised this implosion could be helpful in understanding this new spiritual phenomenon.

Baudrillard and Hyper-Reality

For the young Baudrillard, who was at that time a neo-Marxist, consumer society was an extension of productive forces. In his early views of society, consumers' needs and pleasures were constrained and institutionalised. After having socialised the proletarian masses into a labour force, the industrial system went further to fulfil itself and indoctrinated the masses into a force of consumption. Baudrillard argued that consumers of the twentieth century were unconscious and unorganised, just as workers appear to have been at the beginning of the nineteenth century (Baudrillard, 1970; 1988).

However, with the proliferation of communications through the mass media, particularly television, and the full emergence of consumer society, Baudrillard moved away from a neo-Marxist perspective to a postmodern one (e.g. Baudrillard, 1979; 1988; 1983; 1995).

The result of this proliferation, for Baudrillard, is that culture is now dominated by simulations – these are objects and discourses that have no firm origin, no referent, no ground or foundation. In consumer culture, signs get their meanings from their relations with each other, rather than by reference to some independent reality or standard. Baudrillard's theory of commodity culture removes any distinction between objects and representation. In their place he pictures a social world constructed out of models or "simulacra" which have no foundation in any reality except their own. For example, the current theme parks representing Hollywood movies or Mickey Mouse cartoons which are very popular in the western world do not represent "reality" but rather the world of Hollywood. In these parks, the signs on offer have no ground in "reality" but are rather connected to these "Mickey Mouse" worlds of fiction. In the game *Kingdom Hearts* which introduced this chapter, the codes of the game have no clear ground with the "reality" as constructed in the fantasy genre, but with the commodified Disneyesque worlds. Daytime television viewers, according to Baudrillard, tend to speak about soap opera characters rather than "real" people. Indeed, how many times have we been speaking about characters from movies and/or television series, rather than "real" people? Myself, for example, have moved towards this trend when I lecture. I tend to speak about movies and their characters when illustrating diverse sociological and philosophical theories rather then "real" life stories and characters. Popular news broadcasts are now more about entertainment than information about "real" social issues; this process has even been called "infotainment". In the world of news, "reality" is adapted for the screen to be consumed. For this reason, Baudrillard, in a sarcastic fashion, claimed that the Gulf War from the early 1990s never happened because it was visually created for the television – e.g. computer simulation, manipulation of images, etc., before any event took place in Iraq. The theory is that these days, the "model" precedes the event and exhausts it totally in advance; this means that behind this virtuality the "real" event is nowhere to be seen.

In this society of spectacles – that is, a society in which social relationships between people are mediated by images (Debord, 1995) – there is no fixed meta-code. Modern society is saturated by images with the media generating a "non-material", or "de-materialised" concept of reality. It seems we live in an economy of signs in which signs are exchanged against each other rather than against the real. To express this idea, Baudrillard uses the metaphor of the Moebius strip (Figure 1) in which there is no beginning or end. Signs and symbols on this strip are all connected to each other without knowing how they started to represent reality or what they will end up symbolising. They are part of an on-going process of feeding on each other in a permanent state of flux.

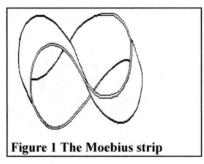

Figure 1 The Moebius strip

If Marx's vision of society was a giant workhouse, Baudrillard's vision is that modern society is now structured by signs and symbols in which it becomes difficult to distinguish the real from the unreal: from this, hyper-reality – that is, a situation in which reality has collapsed – takes over. We can take as examples the Imax theatres which make us feel at a certain place without having to travel. We can now visit Mount Everest and feel it through these images without encountering an ascetic voyage. Further, the images that are created for the viewers that become "reality" become what this place is, and the "real reality" that is not showed (e.g. long waiting hours, smell of sweat, pollution on the side of the panoramic view) does not become part of our conceptions. It is easy to think of a kid who saw a place/building on television and who, confronted with the "real" place, does not think it is "real"; that it is not like the one on the television. In pornography, the images that are shown create a new kind of reality about sex (Baudrillard, 1979). In those movies, close-ups of certain positions – that we are not able to see while we make love (at least for me who is not a contortionist) – are creating a sense of reality that becomes more real than reality – that is, hyper-real – just by showing everything.

This vision accurately portrays current western postmodern times in which people seem to seek spectacle more than meaning. Indeed, as explored in the previous chapter, some spiritual consumers are inspired by horror stories (e.g. H.P. Lovecraft), science fiction stories (e.g. *Star Wars, Star Trek*, etc.), and fantasy stories (e.g Tolkien and his *Lord of the Rings*) to support their subjective myths.

This hyper-real phenomenon has some implications, not only on the spiritual consumers' subjective myth, but also on how they see themselves; that is, their identification. This has been touched lightly above with Jediknightism. Identification to a Jedi Knight by a spiritual consumer might be an inspiration to the spiritual actor to develop their self and tap into latent forms of powers from within the self. It can thus be argued that today the source of identification does not have to be part of the real world but can also be hyper-real. In this, we can see the interactions between the field of fiction and the self in this hyper-real world. This will be developed in the next chapter.

By hyper-real religion I thus refer to a simulacrum of a religion partly created out of popular culture which provides inspiration for believers/consumers at a metaphorical level. This religion is still embryonic at the moment, however we can expect a growth in the near future as we move towards a post "September 11th 2001" risk society.

Hyper-Real Religion in the Risk Society

Not only have we moved towards a postmodern society, but we also live in a risk society (Beck, 1992). It appears that since humans have secularly taken control of nature (industrialisation) and themselves (emancipation), risk, which at one time was the responsibility of an omnipotent God (e.g. war, famine, plague), would now be the sole responsibility of human kind. In the early days of industrialisation, risks were evident to the senses – they could be smelt, touched, tasted or observed with the naked eye (e.g. explosion in a factory). These risks were evaluated, predicted and calculable. In contrast many of the major risks today largely escape perception and calculation, for they are localised in the sphere of physical and chemical formulas (e.g. toxins in foodstuffs or the nuclear threat). They are no longer constrained within the constructed boundaries of nation states; indeed, the explosion of Chernobyl has affected diverse countries in the world and we are still suffering from the unknown consequences of this accident.

Risk is now dissolved in the minute, yet innumerable, traps and ambushes of daily life. One tends to hear it knocking now and again, daily, in fatty fast food, in listeria-infected eggs, in cholesterol rich temptations, in sex without condoms, in cigarette smoke, in asthma-inducing carpet mites, in the dirt you see and the germs you do not. (Bauman, 1998: 65)

Living in such a society affects people's sense of their self, and can increase their existential anxiety, or as it is also called, their ontological insecurity; that is, an obsessive exaggeration of risks to personal existence, extreme introspection and moral vacuity. The opposite of that state of being is ontological security; that is, a sense of reliability of persons and things aided and abetted by the predictability of the (apparent) minor routines of day-to-day life. It incorporates trust in the reliability of persons and things. Trust, therefore, may be regarded as a means of dealing psychologically with risks that would otherwise paralyse action or lead to feelings of engulfment, dread and anxiety.

However, with the shift towards postmodernity, trust is no longer based on traditions. As explored previously, our world is now characterised by transformations in traditional habits and customs. People now cannot simply rely on local knowledges, tradition, religious precepts, habit or observation of others' practices, such as those from parents and school teachers, to conduct their everyday lives, as they did in early modern times. As explored with the *à la carte* consumption of religion, spiritual consumers construct their subjective myths and thus, to a certain extent, rely on themselves. Human knowledge and beliefs are thus lacking foundations and might create uncertainty and a desire for stability, certainty and predictability. Furthermore as Giddens (1991) claims about the current western population at large, we are on our own and thus our lives have become more insecure. We might have greater freedom but we also have more personal responsibility for managing our own lives. This can create a sense of insecurity.

We might think that in the postmodern world, where there has been a general collapse of certainties – e.g. family life, job security, and sexuality – we are more tolerant of difference. This is indeed true. We no longer crave the modernist dream to normalise, we no longer long to tame or correct the "other". However, this increased fragmentation means that our insecurities – often distorted – are projected elsewhere.

This society which is prone to risks (risk society) and fragmentation (postmodernity) has recently been amplified by the event of September the 11th, 2001. These events have already been theorised (e.g. Armitage, 2002; Beck, 2002; Bendle, 2002; Encel, 2002; Hoffmann, 2002; McDonald, 2002) and could herald the beginning of a new era and paradigm. Beck (2002) even states that September 11th stands for the complete collapse of language, since we have problems using current concepts to describe what happened. He believes that the perception of terrorist threats "triggers a self-multiplication of risks by the de-bounding of risk perception and fantasies" (Beck, 2002: 44). This has many implications and this section will focus instead on the expected development of one trend that could affect these hyper-real forms of consumption in this post-September 11th "risk society". The main form of religion that is directly affected by these changes is of course Islam – the major target of an increase of fear and anxiety –, however, this is not a topic under scrutiny in this chapter. The remaining of this section is purely speculative and presents merely a possible future scenario. I do this in the hope of stimulating discussion and enquiry rather than providing conclusions.

Since the 1960s there has been a growing move away from institutionalised religions which favoured the development of new religious movements such as The Church of Scientology, the Church of All Worlds, and the Church of Satan. This created a platform which allowed the more individualistic beliefs and practices found in New Age and neo-paganism to develop from the 1980s. In his analysis of different surveys of the American population since September 2001, Etzioni (2002) concludes that Americans have become more spiritual – but not more active in organised religion. The September 11th violence and its mediatisation might not only increase this shift towards more religious individualism but it might even give a support to the development of a new form of religion that is still embryonic at the moment, and which we have just addressed: the hyper-real religion. Indeed, if we have experienced in the period from 1960 to today a move from a form of individualism towards a form of narcissism as expressed in the literature on postmodernity (e.g. Lipovetsky, 1987; 1993), we might expect the future Narcissus to stop looking at himself, and to look instead at an image of himself as portrayed and tamed in the media and popular culture; that is, a hyper-real image of himself – a hyper-real subjective myth.

How should we interpret this growing move towards hyper-real religion if it happens? Coming back to an understanding of what popular culture is would be a good starting point to answer this question.

Bar-Haim (1990: 281) suggests that

The wide range of popular culture phenomena are generated at the expense of dominant belief systems such as ideology, religion, various forms of spiritual movements, and the like – often for the purpose of suggesting their inadequacy or bankruptcy.

Within this view, popular culture, it is suggested, comments on ideo-logical effects without necessarily proposing a realistic nor utopian alternative (Bar-Haim, 1990: 285). It does provide "symbolic and expressive commentaries to those everyday living concerns that emanate from ideological imperatives" (Bar-Haim, 1990: 280), and these can be expressed as forms of escapism and/or as rituals of resistance. These two forms will now be addressed in the light of hyper-real religion.

Would hyper-real religion be a form of escapism that would allow spiritual consumers to move away from "real" religions and their per-ceived violence; that is, a move toward a popular culture that is less confrontational than reality? In this instance, "Unreal" religion might bring more comfort to certain religious actors. Indeed, apart from the writing of Lovecraft, in which the hero tends to loose his mind after encountering the mysterious, the works of popular culture which tend to be used as a support for hyper-real religion have very often as a plot the defeat of evil by the good; or when the evil is not defeated, it might give to the consumer a sense of awe (e.g. desire to become a vampire). These stories are more comforting than a reality in which an army has been sent to a country to defeat a network of Muslim terrorists and is still – in the time of writing – looking for what it seems to be the unstoppable.

Or would hyper-real religion be a form of protest against mainstream culture as found in some life-affirming Latin American popular relig-ions? In these popular religions, we find the expression of the marginal-ised, the demonised and the dominated. Popular religion in this instance "provides the dominated with a space for the perpetuation of their threatened culture by protecting against assimilative forces, and func-tioning as a vehicle of social empowerment" (Mejido, 2002: 305). With these hyper-real religions, we might expect the same type of protest but not necessarily from a marginalised, demonised and dominated strata of Western societies; but what specific type of protest? As part of this protest, we could perhaps find an affirmation of a desire to live and experience life in a socio-economic and political context that puts people at risk (Parker, 1998). This view of popular religion is specific to certain cases in Latin America, however, it is tempting to link popular religion with hyper-religion for a while and argue that hyper-real relig-ion might be also a support to affirm life in a risk society. As religion in general (Possamai-Inesedy, 2002), hyper-real religion and its subjective myths could perhaps provide a sense of ontological security to its con-sumer.

If we come back to the example of *Star Wars* which introduced this chapter, we found in Australia that it was estimated that about 5,000 people would be true "hard-core" people that would believe the

Jedi Religion. It might be possible to argue that while the *Star Wars* mythos provides them with a source of inspiration for their subjective myths, also, in this post-September 11th risk society, it might provide a source of escapism as well. Believing at a metaphorical level to gain the powers of a Jedi Knight might provide a more interesting route to self-development than the diverse routes from mainstream religion and their perceived lack of relevance to everyday life and their perceived fanaticism. For the remaining people who declared *Star Wars* to be their religion, if they do or do not use this mythos for their subjective myths, they might have used the Census as a form of protest against the government; or just for fun.

However, even if Jediism is an outcome of the *Star Wars* series, it does not mean that some social actors want to see it turning into a more established religion adapted to our contemporary world. As the Internet site on *Becoming Jediism* underlines:

> It is not the intention of our organisation to be yet another container for a whole of creation, yet another paradigm which limits the true release of the Force, and interfere with the soul becoming One with the Will of the Force. That is counterproductive and would not allow the growth of the theology of Jediism. We offer an alternative to the many religions and philosophical movements that are available, and it is our solemn belief that Jediism is soon forming into a viable religion and inner faith to lead those willing to submit themselves firmly upon the path of knowledge to what we call a spiritual renaissance which can take the Jedi much higher into the world of spirit and embrace much higher truths than any that were ever conjured up from the science fiction series.[8]

Perhaps we could interpret this "spiritual renaissance" as a growth of hyper-real religion that wants to stay away from any structure and is a form of escapism and contestation, but also an affirmation of life in this risk society.

---

[8]   Internet site, http://www.jediism.org/generic/html?pid=0 (7/03/03).

CHAPTER 5

New Forms of Religious Identification Carried by Popular Culture

Introduction

In the movie *Wolf*, the middle-aged Jack Nicholson has turned into a werewolf. At the start of his curse, he was scared of his new self and hoped to cure his "malediction"/"disease". Seeking a rational explanation for his condition, he finds an expert – a retired scholar of the mysterious. The ageing expert, knowing about the new strength, the new powers and the regained youth of Nicholson, asks, in a non sado-masochist voice, to be bitten by him. He hopes by this to be turned into a werewolf, to regain youth and strength and to receive some animalistic and powerful abilities.

Blade, originally a Marvel Comics series adapted for the larger screen, is half vampire and half human. He was born from a mother who turned vampire just before giving birth and who transmitted her newly received powers to her son. The hero has kept the power of the vampire but can nevertheless walk during the day without being affected by the sun. He is thus called a "day walker". In this movie, Blade has set the task to get rid of a vampire tribal leader, Deacon Frost, whose dream is to convince all vampires to take over the world instead of hiding in gothic places as they have been doing for centuries. Frost commands not only vampires from his clan, but also humans who have the craving to become vampires. They are discreetly marked like cattle and are helping vampires during the day in the hope that one day, after having satisfied their master(s), they could be emptied of their blood. In this movie, certain characters are ready to give their human nature to gain power and immortality.

The sub-texts of these two movies underline a desire by some human characters for out-of-the-ordinary power, be it physical or psychic. This is part of the realm of fiction, but what if it could apply to the everyday life of some consumers of popular culture? The exploration of the

Midichlorians debate from the *Star Wars* series might help us to move closer to reality.

The first three episodes of the *Star Wars* series that were released in the 1970s and 1980s (*Star Wars*, *The Empire Strikes Back* and *The Return of The Jedi*) have as a sub-text the theme of the Force. Here are two quotes from these movies:

> Obi Wan: Remember, a Jedi can feel the Force flowing through him.
> Luke: You mean it controls your actions?
> Obi Wan: Partially. But it also obeys your commands.
> Yoda: For my ally is the Force, and a powerful ally it is. Life creates it, makes it grow. Its energy surrounds us and binds us. Luminous beings we are, not this crude matter.

This sub-text of the Force, as a type of energy that can be tapped into, has attracted many enthusiastic consumers of the *Star Wars* mythos. By obeying it, one is able to predict events, control gravity, be a telekinesist, influence people's minds... For example, as one fan explains in a discussion list:

> To me [...], this implies that Force-users are special because they are able to tap into this "higher-power", if you will, through intense training and dedication (much like the samurai and other warriors in Chinese and Japanese folklore), not because little things in their blood tell them to.

These "little things in someone's blood" have created a controversy among *Star Wars* fans. In the *Phantom Menace*, the fourth movie made and the first of the series, the sub-text of the Force becomes slightly different. The Jedi Knight, Qui Gon, to check if a young boy – the one who will later become Darth Vader – has the Force, tests the young blood and finds an excessive amount of Midichlorians; i.e. some microscopic life forms, especially numerous in a Jedi's blood, that are scientifically – and not spiritually – believed to communicate with the Force. These Midichlorians are used to explain in the movie the young Darth Vader's natural ability to connect with the Force. In other words, and contrary to what the first three movies made the viewer believe, one must now be born a Jedi in order to take the Jedi's inner journey; one can no longer become one. This has created some lengthy discussion on an Internet site:[1]

> As soon as blood samples are taken, everything becomes scientific and NOT spiritual. Do I have blood tests to see how strong my Catholic faith is? A spiritual thing cannot be analysed and compared with other people. It is something inside you. Keeping the force vague is what made it interesting.

---

[1]   Internet site, http://boards.theforce.net/The_Phantom_Menace (04/02/2005).

It was officially the single worse concept Georgie boy [Georges Lucas] came up with.

But anyone can become a Catholic but it was apparent that not everyone can be a Jedi. There had to be a reason and with cloning being an issue in future episodes maybe GL [Georges Lucas] HAD to say why some people have it and some people don't.

In this debate there is first a surprise that to become a Jedi Knight you have to be biologically predestined. This leads to another sub-debate in which there are questions about the spiritual side of these Midichlorians, especially if they need to be discovered scientifically – use of a blood test – instead of through a spiritual path. From the debate, it comes out that most fans do not believe that Midichlorians have necessarily replaced the spiritual side of the Force with a scientific explanation only. Rather, there is a forming consensus that a higher count of Midichlorians would allow a Jedi Knight to be able to form a communication with the Force; that is, both obeying and commanding it. For those who have a low count of Midichlorians, the Force still exists and surrounds them, but it does not give them any super-powers. Even if there is a sense of a consensus among *Star Wars* fans from this discussion list, many of them are left somewhat frustrated that one has to be born a Jedi Knight and can no longer become one.

From these examples, it becomes tempting to argue for a plausible connection between the desire of acquiring super powers and popular culture. One way to analyse this affinity is by exploring the birth of the character of a new mythos that has enabled new types of characters – including Jedi Knights – to emerge in popular culture, and through this, might have created a new type of elective affinity with consumers of popular culture: the birth of Superman in 1938. This will soon be addressed after an ex-cursus on postmodern identities.

A World of Multiple Possibilities

According to Elliot (2001: 158), postmodern theorists argue that the world has led to "the culture and consumption of new identities, in which the free flight of fantasy appears in everything from self-help manuals to TV chat-shows". As Melucci (1996: 31) explains, we are nomads of the present, without our identity having a set of given or inherited characteristics; there is instead a "processual, self-reflexive, and constructed manner in which we define ourselves". Identity tends to be associated in this context with a thirst for reinvention, reconstruction, restaging and reshaping that can also be based on fantasy and phantasmagoria.

In this consumer world of multiple cultural possibilities, could this hyper-real world lead to new identifications and/or fantasies that are shared, consciously or unconsciously, by people at large? This chapter investigates the popularisation of the belief in the human potential ethic (a term coined in Possamai, 2001b) – that is, a belief in the spiritual development of the self and its latent abilities – and compares it with the development of superheroes in comics. This is done in order to highlight the interrelation between the fields of popular culture and that of religion. I suggest that the affinity between superheroes in comics and this human potential ethic refers to an intimate co-existence of these two elements and not to a relationship of cause and effect (see Weber, 1968).

As expressed in the following extract found in a New Age magazine on the Internet, we discover how a person makes a link with superheroes, and the assumption that we all have latent abilities.

[…] When I was a young boy, I recall playing superheroes with my younger brother, in our back yard. We would declare our powers and use them to our benefit, of course; and it all seemed "real" in a sense […] even if it were in our imaginations. Funny thing is though, now that I am older and have come to terms with certain gifts I have; actually that we all have; I have come to realize that with these powers comes a decent amount of responsibility and compassion.

In comparing the gifts I have become familiar with and comfortable using, it is the empathic one that still remains the hardest to adjust to. Everyone is born an empath and continues throughout life utilizing empathic abilities. What we call hunches, a vibe, a gut feeling, and in some cases even when we simply rely on instinct; all of these stem from empathy. Defined, empathy regards the ability to share in another person's emotions, thoughts, and feelings. In a spiritual sense however, we all do this. It is a natural born gift. I am sure we have experienced a moment when we accuse someone of bringing our spirits down or up. This can be accredited to an empathic ability […]

Who would have guessed that the ability to become a superhero is innate in us. All we have to do is acknowledge it, trust it, and then utilize it.[2]

The Human Potential Ethic and Alternative Spiritualities

This ethic – even if already present for a long time among esoteric groups in western societies (Faivre, 1992) – corresponds to the evolution of the Human Potential Movement whose origins "may be traced to sensitivity training in the late 1940s" (Stone, 1976: 95). From this

---

[2]   O. Yeldell, "The role of the Empath", *Of Spirit.com: Healing Body, Mind & Spirit*, Internet site, http://www.ofspirit.com/omaryedldell1.htm (04/02/04).

followed the study of group dynamics and interpersonal problem solving which became a nationwide movement in the 1960s. It is in the 1970s that the name Human Potential Movement (Stone, 1976:96) came into use. From this time period, eastern disciplines were adapted to western settings, and this movement developed its emphasis on transpersonal and spiritual experience. There was a shift from a work of self-transcendence of going beyond the routines of everyday life to the self-transcendence of merging with spiritual energies. In this Human Potential Movement, groups such as Humanistic Psychology (e.g. Maslow and Fromm) are found with spiritual groups such as Est, Zen meditation, and the alternative spiritualities under investigation.

People following this ethic find in the soul something similar to, or even identical with, divine Reality and this is discovered by an inner adventure. They can find a divine spark within themselves which could lead to a spiritual mutation. This potential includes greater insight, body awareness, and communication with others. It leads to personal growth and development of latent abilities as the New Age quote above illustrates. This is often presented in the "New Age" literature in the expression: "You are god and can do anything".

There are various terms expressing this inner adventure. There is the description of a Jivanmukta in Smith (1989: 253-256), or Eliade's "coincidentia oppositorium" and his portrait of an androgyne (Eliade, 1962); or Jung's "process of individuation"; or René Guénon's (1958) "universal man".

This inner adventure is not necessarily that of searching to become a god, or a super human, but it can be understood as the realisation of a "higher" self. By understanding one's body/mind/spirit, by operating on the self through meditation, preventive healing, or other praxes, it is possible to develop one's self. As seen previously, this reflects a heuristic spectrum which could be clarified defining one side as the quest for an instrumental development – which refers to some techniques an individual uses to better himself or herself to become more effective and efficient in worldly pursuits, e.g. use of yoga to release stress. And the other side reflects a search for illuminational development; that is, a quest for a direct inner personal experience of the divine within, or for a greater individual potential, e.g. use of yoga for meditation.

This ethic is not necessarily confined to a minority culture. It also permeates mainstream culture. As an example, Ross (1991: 27) realises that these "alternative" orientations are found in mainstream talk shows, such as the *Oprah Winfrey Show*, which is not avowed as being part of these spiritualities but popularises certain principles such as growth and potential. We will come back to this show in a later section of this chapter.

Superheroes in Comics

> The assertion is that comic books in the postwar decade, through a unique combination of text and pictures, offered a world-view to a large segment of the American population [...] that did not as yet have one. The world after 1945, as historians are wont to say, was a more confusing place than it had ever been before; and Americans generally were at some pains to explain their position in it. Comic books, like other products of mass culture, comprised one vehicle for explanation. (Savage, 1990: ix)

Before coming back to the postwar decade, it is essential to draw attention to the "Golden Age" of comics in America which started with the debut of *Superman* in 1938. Savage (1990: 6) establishes that as a cultural artefact, the Superman character, gained an enormous audience, not only in comics but in other media such as animated cartoons, radio and television. The creation of this character also laid down the norms and conventions of the other super-heroic characters that were about to come. Readers asked for more, comic artists had to follow the demand and consequently the superhero market boomed.

However, the superhuman theme first appeared in American science fiction around the beginning of the twentieth century, but was seen positively only with the arrival of *Superman* in 1938. Before that, "the message of the superman stories [was] always the same: whether saviour or destroyer, the superman cannot be permitted to exist" (Andrea, 1987: 125). The author also discusses the Nietzschean concept of the *Übermensch* glorifying Aryan racial superiority, which was perceived as negative in the superman theme in American science fiction. Another reason is that in a world dominated by a Christian ethos, the belief in becoming a god was blasphemy.

But Superman, the comic book creation, became a cultural icon because

> he is the embodiment of society's noblest ideals, a "man of tomorrow" who foreshadows mankind's highest potentialities and profoundest aspirations but whose tremendous powers, remarkably, pose no danger to its freedom and safety. (Andrea, 1987: 125)

By the 1940s, comic books were being published in greater quantities, and new superheroes were constantly appearing. Superheroes had virtually taken over the comic book medium because of the economic success of the Superman mythos (McAllister, 1990: 58). During the World War II, comics were reinforcing dominant social values in the

USA, and superheroes were mainly fighting against the Axis menace (Savage, 1990; McAllister 1990). By 1946-1947, Savage (1990: 12-13) argues, the superhero comic genre had exhausted the dramatic possibilities of its stories, and a new socio-cultural climate arose after Hiroshima. Only *Superman, Batman* and *Wonder Woman* continued to be published. Crime comics, western comics, war comics, satire comics and horror/science fiction comics became more fashionable (Reynolds, 1992: 8). Following the excess of the horror comics came the widely read account by the New York psychiatrist, Fredric Wertham (1996) who, in *Seduction of the Innocent*, portrayed comic books as dangerous. This report caused great alarm amongst parents and politicians and a severe censorship of the comics industry soon followed. Consequently, the number of comic books sold in newsagents dropped from around 650 in 1953-1954 to around 250 in 1956 (Savage, 1990: 100). A Comics Code Authority was designed to counter act this moral attack and, by doing so, "mainstream" the values and messages presented in comic books (McAllister, 1990). Paradoxically, book publishers rediscovered the costumed superheroes: they were morally acceptable to the "innocent" and were economically viable. Publishing houses decided to resuscitate and re-costume some of its superheroes of the golden age, such as Flash in 1956 and Green Lantern in 1959. This was the so-called "Silver Age" of comics, this name referring to the new development of the superheroes' mythos and the promotional effort of Stan Lee and Marvel Comics; e.g. with *Spiderman* and the *Fantastic Four* (Daniels, 1991: 82-145).

The religious underpinning in the superman mythos exists and it had, I argue, an impact on the popularisation of the human potential ethic. The connection between comics and religion has been addressed in *Superman* (Reynolds, 1992) and *Silver Surfer* (Gabilliet, 1994), but has been mainly connected to biblical imagery. Savramis (1987) goes further into the religious analysis of Superman and discovers, Christian elements aside, references to suprasensible forces found in what he calls occultism, which have a strong affinity with the human potential ethic. Schechter (1979) and Hodge (1988) make reference to some aspects of popular culture which serve a "magico-religious" function as premodern mythologies used to do; there would even be a submerged spiritual significance in comics' superheroes. It is my contention that by turning super powers from the comics medium into commodities and thus being widely accessed by people, it created an unintended consequence in western consumer culture, that of being in affinity with, and popularising, the human potential ethic. In other words, Superman, as argued before, being the first character with positively stigmatised superpowers in popular culture, has built what I call, an "imaginary doxa", i.e. a general desire grounded in everyday life fantasies which has been created by works of fiction. We could imagine specific forms of "imaginary doxa" – that is, as wanting to be beautiful and wealthy like certain soap opera characters, or as being as sexually active as certain characters in pornographic movies, or as being as skinny as certain models in magazines. In the case of this chapter, this "imaginary doxa" is used by people to attempt to, consciously or not, acquire and/or achieve superpowers. This "doxa" is not part of a force of production attempting to make people cultural dupes; writers and producers of these superhero stories did not set out consciously to produce and/or re-enforce this human potential ethic.[3] The thesis here is not a simple one of emulation, such as a reader wanting to look like a superhero, but more of a metaphysics of transformation in the reader's mind. This "doxa" would rather be part of a "fantasy collective" – and here I para-phrase Durkheim's notion of conscience collective. This fantasy created by works of fiction – a space where affective relationships and identities can be articulated – makes people dream, and makes them wish for some out-of-worldly outcomes, and might, to a certain extent, influence people's everyday lives. Indeed, "as directors of our own self-narratives, we draw upon psychic frames of memory and desire, as well as wider cultural and social resources, in fashioning [ourselves]" (Elliot, 2001: 2). In this "imaginary doxa", the development of superheroes in comics and the popularisation of the desire to reach a "super" self, i.e. the following of a human potential ethic, are in affinity. This, I argue, might have helped to re-enforce a belief in people to gain (super) abilities in their spiritual and/or everyday life.

Baby Boomers and Generation X

In the USA, the baby boomers bought for a dime the latest exploits of the superheroes after WWII, and they were those who were first brought up in this mass consumption of comics. However, they were more than merely a generation inspired by comics (Daniels, 1991: 89-94), they were also more responsive to new ideas than their parents (Beckford and Levasseur, 1986: 33). The more educated young were less committed to life-long engagement such as marriage and work than their parents: their spending power was greater, they were keen to

---

[3]   Salisbury (1999) interviewed fourteen leading Anglo-Saxon comics scriptwriters, and only two made direct references to religion. The only specific comment that is con-nected to the thesis of this chapter is expressed by Grant Morrison: "JLA (a group of superheroes) is full of mythological references and folk tale stuff, but nobody needs to know about it. If you do know about it, it will enrich your reading, but if you don't know about it you'll still get a rollicking good laugh" (*o.c.*: 212).

experiment with new lifestyles and discover new cultures (*o.c.*: 34). They were the first generation to be affected by television and feel the impact of mass communication. It is not difficult to show affinities between the experience of freedom, the loosing of social structures, and the increasing range of options of the baby boomers, such as discovering underground and eastern spiritualities supporting a belief in the human potential ethic.

I am tempted to claim that this generation – at least in the Anglo-Saxon world – could have carried this affinity between superheroes in comics and the human potential ethic, and that it could have also made it available to other generations.

In other parts of the western world, the superhero mythos and its translation only appeared in the late 1960s and mainly affected Generation X. For example, in 1949 in France came the law on youth publications signed during the Cold War. This law led to the auto-censorship of some publishing houses of material going against the sixteen articles of the law, especially its second article which forbids any story supporting criminality, lying, theft, laziness, cowardice, hate, debauchery, or other acts which could lead to a demoralised youth. The commission put into place to administer this law asked for some local productions to be re-worked or, very rarely, to be removed, but these were in the minority compared to the pressure put on American titles. Indeed, the American comics, especially the western, gangster and superhero genres were seen as supporting violent discourses which needed to be canalised. *Tarzan* and the *Phantom* were the epitome of these stories which were going against the 1949 law. As an outcome of this pressure, it became risky and non profitable to publish these types of transatlantic publications.

As part of that commission were representatives of diverse social groupings, including those of local publishers and artists who have militated since 1936 in favour of a state protectionism against foreign publications, and those of the communist party[4] fighting for the anti-Americanisation of the French culture. Indeed, since 1945 the American dollar from the Marshall Plan has occupied the French economic landscape; and American Jazz, cinema, crime fiction, and science fiction has dominated the mass French culture (Ory, 1999: 71).

Even if not explicitly stated in the law and in the various reports from this commission, the outcome of this censorship led to a cultural protection against American popular culture. Although the American imports were cheaper to publish in the Francophone world, the politics

---

[4] On top of this, the French communist party also had its comics magazine in circulation; it was first called "*Vaillant*" and later "*Pif (gadget)*".

had, in this case, taken control of the market (Crépin and Groensteen, 1999). This allowed the local comics genre to emerge after World War II, especially the comics from Belgium – known as the Belgian School (Sabin, 1996; Screech, 1999) – where publishing houses (e.g. *Dupuis, Casterman* and *Le Lombard*) were already following a paternalistic and Catholic auto-censorship in connection to the different articles of the law before its advent.

It is very tempting to argue that this case in the western world might be one of the first attempts to fight against globalisation and its mono and hegemonic culture, as epitomised by American mass culture. This censorship process apparently had the benefit of boosting the local creativity, to offer new narratives in the vast global library of comics, and to allow a form of expression not dominated by the superhero mythos as it is now in the Anglo-Saxon culture.

It is only in the late 1960s that these comics were translated and published monthly in the francophone world. However, if the superhero mythos was not offered to the first baby boomers from the continent while they were children, it nevertheless permeated through the American science fiction literature.

The Human Potential Ethic and Superheroes in Affinity: Three Arguments

Before WWII, the idea of a human being being able to reach a "higher self" was, if culturally accessible, mostly maintained in "High Culture", and thus limited to an elite; whereas in "Low Culture", superhuman powers – before Superman – were, as argued before, pejoratively described. There have always been works of art supporting and rendering plausible a discourse on the human potential ethic (Faivre, 1992; Henderson, 1987), however, what is important and new, is that these works promoting the human potential ethic are now constituents of popular/consumer culture.

I believe there are three reasons why superheroes in comics were one of various agents of popularisation of the human potential ethic:

First, the character of Superman innovated a double non-problematic personality – a kind of benign Dr. Jekyll and Mr. Hyde in the form of Clark Kent/Superman (aka Kal-El) – and became a characteristic of reference for the superheroes to come. This double life of the superhero allows him or her to be exceptional, but not exceptional enough to be cast out by his or her society. As Wedgwood (1930: 139) writes, inspired by the excursus of Simmel (1991: 52-63) on ornamentation:

In every individual there are two conflicting impulses: the one to resemble his fellows; the other to be different from them. Human beings are gregarious but they are also individualists. While everyone wishes to remain within the community, every normal individual desires to be in some degree outstanding in that community.

As Andrea (1987) discovers: "Superman differs from his predecessors in science fiction by being able to exist within society by disguising himself as the self-deprecating and mild-mannered Clark Kent"; a down-to-earth middle-class American man whom readers can relate to in everyday life'. Superman became popular in comics because his powers were positively perceived; but just as importantly, his dual identity means that he does not need to give up his role in mainstream society.

Second, superpower, in pre-industrial societies, was generally acquired by divine intervention – you are born a hero or a half-god –, or if it was achieved, the hero had to go through an ascetic initiation to earn it (e.g. Ulysses and Hercules). Whereas in the superhero mythos, superpowers are mainly achieved by accident, i.e. a non-ascetic self-transformation – e.g. Spiderman, the Fantastic Four, with some exceptions such as Batman[5] – or acquired without a divine intervention – e.g. mutants like the X-men. Instead of divine intervention, there is instead a secular usage of contemporary technologies – sometimes willingly, other times by accident involving chemicals, atomic energy, high tech machines, etc, that inadvertely created the superhero (e.g. the Hulk and Flash).

These non-ascetic and secular characters fit with the *Zeitgeist* of a society of leisure which requires quick access to both material and spiritual goods. As Bauman (1998) argues on one facet of postmodern religion, today's seekers of peak-experience consume sensations rather than follow the more ascetic path of "ordinary" seekers of peak-experience (e.g. traditional Buddhist meditation and religious fasting). This builds a plausibility structure for the "imaginary doxa" of "quickly" acquiring super powers without following an ascetic path.

However, there are exceptions. Not every superhero epitomises the notion of quickly-gained powers. Batman is an example of a superhero whose abilities are gained, not by accident or divine intervention, but by years of ascetic training. His motivation in doing so is to solve the psychic trauma stemming from the murder of his parents. However, the young colourfully-dressed Robin was created to contrast with the

---

[5]   Even the identity of Thor, a Norse god, is given to Donald Blake, a MD with a limp, by accident.

gloomy dark Batman and to serve as a source of identification for young adolescents (Brody, 1995). Daredevil is also an ascetic figure, but his super-sensibilities were gained by a "secular" accident before his training.

Third, before superheroes in comics, there were also other heroes – some of whom had superpowers – who were agents of spreading the human potential ethic.

> Tales of heroic endeavour have been popular from time immemorial, and some of the world's most influential narratives have invited readers and listeners to admire, emulate and/or measure themselves against the deeds, attitudes and beliefs of the great and famous. (Grixti, 1994: 214)

Grixti then lists Gilgamesh, Ulysses, Hercules, prophets and religious leaders, and even political and military figures such as Che Guevara, Napoleon Bonaparte and Alexander the Great.

However, these heroes were – if I can generalise – leaders and this status is put into question in today's western society. The rejection of external authority started in the counter-culture of the 1960s with young adults viewing scientists as a new kind of corruption (Roszak, 1969: 262-263). As Kellehear (1996: 97) notes, a wider critique of roles and statuses in modern society was involved in this:

> The belief in the value neutrality of science is long gone, together with unconditional reliance on the local doctor, lawyer, teacher, and parson.

There was a growing scepticism towards institutional authority. The "given", the "traditional" answers supplied by what Voyé (in Roof *et al.*, 1995), inspired by Lyotard, calls the bearer of "Grand Narratives", would be questioned or ignored. Many of the educated young would no longer accept the "set menu" of canonical knowledge.

Eco (1976: 37-39) points out that superheroes, given their abilities, could fight more for political and/or environmental issues. However, they mainly focus their activity on the enforcement of justice in their own community – e.g. Superman in Metropolis and Marvel heroes in New York. Indeed, as Frank Miller, a comics scriptwriter/artist says: "It always struck me as odd, considering the strength of editorial cartoons in newspapers, that comic books were so meticulously apolitical, or even worse politically correct" (Salisbury, 1999: 203). Apart from a few exceptions – e.g. Captain America during the Watergate scandal and other more recent DC and Marvel comics characters – superheroes do not appear to support any Grand Narratives except that of fighting crimes in everyday life, i.e. they support the status quo and are not interested in changing society.

If past heroes were representing an external authority, recent super-heroes such as Superman are only heroes of commodity[6] and are not role models for social and political leadership *per se*. What differs from these "traditional" heroes such as Ulysses and superheroes in comics is that superheroes have been turned into a commodity bearing the "ver-nacular" interest of the people and are thus not agents of a Grand Narra-tive. By becoming part of popular culture, these new (super) heroes consequently became agents for the popularisation of the human poten-tial ethic.

The Human Potential Ethic and Superheroes: Two Comments

First, superheroes in comics are not the only narrative form in elec-tive affinity with the human potential ethic. Other narratives are fantasy, horror and science fiction (e.g. *Star Wars* and *Star Trek*); these having started to take off in an impressive way in the late 1960s (Grixti, 1994). For example, as already touched on in Chapter 3, even if the vampire has been popular since the nineteenth century, it has now a strong appeal and arouses a longing for personal/spiritual/occult transformation, some of these characters even becoming Superman-like rescuers. However, it can be argued that Superman was the first character of a new kind and laid down the norms and conventions of the superhero genre in a world no longer strictly dominated by Christian ethics – in which the belief in becoming a god is blasphemy. This influenced the characters to come in science-fiction, horror, fantasy… genres. Arguably, popular culture, which builds an "imaginary doxa" for the reader to tame the supernatu-ral and super powers, is not limited to superheroes in comics.

Second, in this chapter, I referred to superheroes in a generalised way and there are, of course, exceptions to my argument. The Hulk is a case in point. He cannot control his power and his double identity, but he is nevertheless a popular character. However, a stronger affinity with the human potential ethic can be found in the TV version: Dr. Banner turned into the Hulk because he was trying to develop his hidden strengths (Daniels, 1991: 176).

The best epitome of my claim would be Spider-Man, an adolescent who non-ascetically acquired superpowers via a non-divine accident. Its impact as a character in popular culture has already been assessed by Mondello (1976) and has, I argue, created an "imaginary doxa" for

---

[6] Indeed Superheroes' adventures are printed in a serial, which is different from the archetypical pre-industrial heroes whose story was not told (or re-told) each month (Eco, 1976).

readers to crave for superpowers. The perceived breakthrough with Spiderman is the reality of his alter-ego, Peter Parker, who is a "typical" troubled adolescent – and now young adult. Indeed, when the creators (Stan Lee and Steve Ditko) launched their new character, they were looking at giving a sense of inspiration to their readers, rather than a sense of awe.

Another character is Dr. Strange who appeared in 1963. According to Daniels (1991: 116), he was a product of his time, i.e. when mysticism was popular and when a spiritual life was sought after in a counter-culture milieu. However, his solo series did not last until the end of the 1960s. He only got his own series back in 1988 in a time, according to Daniels (*ibid.*) that culture saw the (re)emergence of New Age spiritualities.

Not every superhero builds a positive elective affinity with the human potential ethic, but a large majority of the characters found in the superhero mythos do. It is worth underlining that the D.C. and Marvel universes are large mythic structures in which characters know each other, and often meet – this is known in the trade as a crossover. Even if all superheroes do not carry my claim, characters who would best fit my argument will also appear as guest stars in other series and thus continue to carry the affinity with the human potential ethic outside their allocated magazine.

The Human Potential Ethic and Jediism

I have argued in the previous sections that the birth of Superman in 1938 might have built an imaginary doxa of gaining superpowers and might have been in affinity with the development of alternative spiritualities. However, this remains in the realm of fantasies and nothing concrete, as far as I am aware, has been attempted by social actors to work towards becoming superheroes. But there are concrete cases of influences from science fiction. For example, Julian, from my fieldwork, expressed his path from reading science fiction to spirituality:

> When I was about 8 I used to read science fiction books and I read about this thing called telepathy, and that [...] got me going. I've got the science books giving me ideas about philosophy [...]. I guess when I was about 16 I got very interested in trying to read minds and you know my friends and I used to try and send each other thoughts, and we had a certain amount of success with that.

However, one of today's more apparent phenomenon is that of becoming a Jedi Knight and this is happening mainly on the Internet. Jediism is not a fan community discussing issues from the *Star Wars* movies, but is a global movement expressing itself via the Internet. There is reference in these chat rooms of a Jedi Temple which represents a cyber place where people can learn about this new spirituality. Although it is present in cyberspace, there were records on some old forums (closed in Oct/Nov 2003 due to hosting problems) of an attempt to raise money to establish such a building in the UK and US. Membership is small for a religion, but significant for a chat room – 287 people were registered on the lists on the 18th of January 2004 – however, not everyone contributed to a "serious" discussion on Jedi rituals. On the previous discussion boards, a hierarchy of Jedi ranks could be achieved by members by training in various online courses. A member could progress from a trainee – a person simply required to participate in discussions – to a Jedi Knight – a fully fledged member –, all the way up to High Councillor – a high rank authority recognised by the leaders of the Jedi community. This arrangement was not included as part of the new lists as it was believed that such "other" progression distracted members from their "inner" development.

Perhaps Jediism will grow into a fully organised religion in the near future but this would be hard to predict. Some quotes from the different chat rooms are listed below and can inform us on how some social actors view the concrete way of becoming a Jedi Knight in their everyday life. It is worth noting that no reference has been found by the author on the Midichlorians issue in these specific chat rooms, as introduced in this chapter, and that these spiritual consumers of *Star Wars* believe that one can become a Jedi Knight – one does not have to be born one.

The first quote deals with Jedi Budo: the all inclusive Jedi martial art which brings into existing techniques the power that can be gained from working towards becoming a Jedi Knight.

> Jedi Budo is more than a system of techniques to control the force (ki, chi, qi). It is a mystical journey of Light, a means to integrate body, heart, mind and soul in one focused release in keeping with the Four Quadrants (Physical, Mental, Emotional and Spiritual). [...] Although Jedi Budo covers a broad curriculum including some of the best and most effective techniques found within many of the best martial arts – Kenpo, Kung Fu, Ju Jitsu, Judo, Aikido, Karate, Tae Kwon Do, Tai Chi Ch'uan – it also includes within it the disciplines encompassing mental clarity, emotional solidity, and spiritual awareness.[7]

---

[7]   Internet site, http://www.jedibudo.com/about.html (04/02/2004).

The two following quotes illustrate that becoming a Jedi is not about fighting choreographically with a laser sword, but about being on a path towards self-development:

A Jedi strives to excel physically, mentally, emotionally and spiritually, and can put these in motion instantly (From the Maxims of the Jediism code).[8]

Meditation is essential on the path of Jediism… Meditation is a key which can open the door to higher perception, unlocking the perfect wisdom on our hearts.[9]

Below, we can find some comments from people who have just joined the list and who are interested in following this path.

I've just signed up and become a jediist follower

I've just become a jedi a few days ago and have begun my life under the ways of becoming 1 with the force. I understand that this is not a star wars rip-off site and am quite glad. Jediism makes a huge amount of sense and has already begun to make an impact on my life. I no longer seek new partners or self-privileges. I've begun to offer help to those who need it and oppose those who act for themselves at the expense of others. I'm beginning to meditate and act as I am meant to by the will of all life for the benefit of all life (human or otherwise). I am 14, coming on 15, and I'm beginning 2 already understand the purpose of all that is about me. I would like to thank the creators of this site (www.jediism.net) for opening my eyes and showing me lifes purpose.

If you could take the Samurai, Arthurian knights, even the Babylon 5 Rangers, and meld them into a single "mystic warrior" order you'd get something resembling what Jedi means to me.

… being a Jedi is really a work in progress of improvement in your self and your ability and desire to help others and your self to understand what it is they should do based on what they want, and if what they want is something that they should want.

The last quote reflects perfectly well this consumer world. In it we find a neo-pagan/witch expressing a strong affinity with Jediism:

Wiccan Jedi

Hi everyone! I recently found out about Jediism, read, and Re-read the website and decided that I love Jediism :-)) I am actually Wiccan, but as Jediist's morals are excellent as well, I decided to merge the two belief systems so I'm a kind of Jedi Witch.

---

8   Internet site, http://www.jediism.org/generic.html?pid=0 (09/09/2004).
9   Internet site, http://www.jediism.org/generic.html;$sessionid$IKH0DHIAAAGLXTZ
ENUGUTIWPERWRJPX0?pid=5 (09/09/2004).

From the exploration of certain Internet sites, it becomes clear that the characters of the Jedi Knights – a type of super-humans – builds an imaginary doxa of developing oneself spiritually and physically. When the spiritual actor moves from the realm of the imaginary doxa to "reality", we see in the case of Jediism that the characters of fiction are adapted to already existing "real" religions as seen in the previous chapter. The label "Jediism" simply becomes a new etiquette for already existing spiritualities and religions, and in that sense, Jediism, in terms of its content, should not be seen as new. This will be explored in a later chapter on the stasis of culture and religion.

Oprah and Spiritual Empowerment

The cases above might been considered at the extreme end of the spectrum of spiritual development; one that is about the (super) development of latent abilities. At the other end of the spectrum, the shows of Oprah Winfrey offer advice on spiritual development, but they do not necessarily involve a radical development of the self as seen previously. In this case, these shows promote empowerment which should be understood as leading someone to a certain control over one's place in daily life by letting that person growth and discover his or her potential.

Parkins (2001) analysed the 1998-1999 season in which a few self-help experts (e.g. John Gray and Suze Orman) made regular appearances. In these shows, an ethics of self-transformation that would facilitate viewers' personal growth and self-improvement was strongly present. This ethics of self-transformation was permeated with a dimension of spirituality encompassing traditional forms of religion as well as what is commonly called New Age philosophy.

Using the language of spirituality for empowerment, comments on the show such as this one were quite strong:

> This "divine discontent" derives from the fact "that you are not living authentically, that you know inside in those quiet moments that you are a magnificent, fabulous, wise, powerful woman and you are not claiming who you are. (Quoted by Parkins, 2001: 151)

> What will start to happen if you say it to yourself enough times, you will be transformed by the language and you will begin to understand that you really are just a spirit inside a body and that the body is the housing-place, it is the temple, but the "who" of who you are is bigger than your body, bigger than your personality, bigger than the things that you will do in your life and the saying of that everyday will help to connect you to it, even if you don't believe it. Even if you don't believe in it. (Quoted by Parkins, 2001: 153)

These quotes reflect the position of women, many of whom are dissatisfied with an absence of purpose despite material and emotional security. They believe that something might be missing and that there is something more to this life than marriage and family. By discussing ways of empowering women, the Oprah show attempts to rebuild the space of the women's everyday life as sacred, as a space for transformation.

The official Internet site for the *Oprah* show has a full section dedicated to spiritual issues titled *Spirit and Self*[10]. Other sections concern *Relationships, Food and Home* and *Mind and Body*. Each section is divided into further subsections on different themes and discussion sections for viewers to discuss their thoughts, do activities and to pose questions. Within the *Spirit and Self* section, we can find the following sub sections; *Know Yourself, Transform Your Life, Inspirations* and *More in Spirit and Self*.

This inner-search for an "authentic" self within a perceived hostile and disempowering everyday life is the focus of discussion. The message tends to emphasise principally a secular ethic of transformation, happiness and success. Here is a quote from one of the participants from one of these discussion lists:

> You are not alone Vicki [In response to a post about an abusive relationship]
> Posted by: susansez
> Posted on: 10/21/2003 at 2:06pm (7.1.1.1.2.2 of 28)
> I am 63, and have been where you are now. But the biggest surprise about abuse was that I was not alone. That you have reached out (through OPRAH) you will find that many have overcome the feelings of "low self esteem" that abuse causes. Have faith that you will Rise Up and see your Divine worth. I have a personal website (osstation.com) that expresses my personal strengths and foibles. I began to post my humor and insights in 1993, and it has been a joy to share with my fellow travellers on Earth. Blessings and Hugs my friend. Susan

The shows of Oprah are but one case out of the many contemporary popular texts promoting self-help, self-improvement and self-transformation. They show us that there are different levels of craving for empowerment, and that included in this specific doxa, there is also a desire for spiritual self-improvement and self-transformation that is not as enchanted as the example from Jediism shows us.

---

[10] Internet site, http://www.oprah.com/spiritself/ss_landing.jhtml (09/09/2004).

A Hyper-Real Re-Enchantment?

This chapter argued first, for a strong elective affinity between the human potential ethic and the development of superheroes in comics, and second, that the appearance of superheroes helped to popularise the belief in reaching the "higher" self. This popularisation was made possible because: 1- the superhero mythos was made attractive to the public via the double identity innovation; 2- fits with a (post)modern *Zeitgeist* – i.e. a non-ascetic acquirement of, and non-divine intervention in giving, superpowers; and 3- is a commodity bearing the "vernacular" interest of the people rather than being an agent of a Grand Narrative.

This elective affinity with superhero comics – and all other characters from popular culture who are a source of inspiration for developing latent abilities – has had the strength of popularising the human potential ethic among alternative spiritualities and in mainstream society. Perhaps it might participate towards a re-enchantment of this world.

Weber saw the changes that drove western society from a traditional to a modern context as a process in which the timeless magic of the universe might be removed and kept outside from a tightly closed iron cage. This, according to Weber, might have reduced human perception and experience of the world to a banal parade of predictable actions in a society of arid routines. Many researchers have commented on the fact that there is a collective move away from the over-rationalisation of everyday life to re-enchanted forms of public and personal spaces. Westerners are facing the return of spiritual/magical thinking in their everyday life which produces a sense of the mysterious, the weird and the uncanny. For Tacey (2000), it is a reconnection with nature – e.g. indigenous landscape – which is at the heart of the re-enchantment process; for Maffesoli (1996), it is the identification with our fellow humans practiced in culture of festivities where people play with their multiple identities. In this sense, it represents "the means by which the hidden or unrecognised powers of human consciousness are made explicit for the purpose of transcending the limits of the secular world... To be re-enchanted means to leave behind the structures that bind individuals to the mundane logic of this world and to reclaim the powers that invigorate the manifestations of other realities" (Lee, 2003: 358).

From this interconnection between religion and popular culture, I would suggest we might be seeing a re-enchantment (*Wiederverzauberung*) from below.[11] For Mike Featherstone (1991: 67-68) and Maffesoli (1996) a feature of the times in advanced western societies (or

---

[11] What Maffesoli (1996: 66) calls a postmodern re-enchantment.

in the global village) is an aestheticisation of everyday life. This is a consequence of the rapid flow of signs and images in contemporary society. Among these signs, which are central to the development of consumer culture, are those of popular culture used by some spiritual actors. For Ritzer (1999), the development of consumer culture itself – with its dizzying proliferation of cathedrals of consumption such as shopping malls, electronic shopping centres, superstores, cruise ships, and casinos – is enchanting our world. These actors, arguably, imbue aestheticised sensibility with a sense of mystery, of invisible power that might be harnessed in consumer and popular culture for human use of enchantment.

In this book so far, we have explored hyper-real religions. Perhaps there is an impact of these religions on re-enchantment narratives. I argue that there is a call to the hyper-real in re-enchantment narratives; that is, a simulacrum created out of, and partly carried by, popular culture. I have already explored elsewhere (Possamai, 2001a) the idea that alternative spiritualities might be re-enchanting parts of our world. However, my aim here is to assess the possibility that elements of popular culture might have a place in this process as well. This chapter has suggested that superhero comics, as a source of popular culture, are not only hyper-real moments but may also contribute to re-enchantment narratives by posing the superhero as an archetypal expression of a greater human potential.

CHAPTER 6

Esoteric Knowledge(s) and Popular Culture

Introduction

In the movie *The Matrix*, Neo (Keanu Reeves) is a computer scientist bored with the routine of his day-to-day job. At night, he is a hacker of international reputation who tries to discover what the Matrix is. The Matrix is at this stage a type of secret knowledge from the cyber-world so well hidden that, like a type of cyber-Eldorado, one wonders if it really exists. One night, in his home office, messed up with a vast array of computer equipment and with a few books scattered around – one written by Baudrillard – exhausted by his illegal activities, he is invited to a discotheque by a woman revealing a tattoo of a white rabbit on her shoulder. This scene is a metaphor of Alice following the white rabbit down the hole and getting to Wonderland; another world beyond the limit of our reality. After a few scenes with some mysterious law en-forcers, Neo meets Morpheus (Laurence Fishburne); the man with the allure of a Zen master who possesses the key to the Matrix. After a quick discussion in a run-down room, Morpheus offers Neo to choose between two pills. The red will give Neo the key to the Matrix and all the answers he has always wanted to know, the blue will prevent him from doing so and will allow him to get back to his everyday life un-changed. After a few moments of hesitation, Neo takes the red pill of knowledge without much regret and discovers with great pain that he never lived in the twentieth century as he thought he had since his birth. This was just an illusion created by Artificial Intelligences to keep humans under a state of permanent control. Breaking away from this cyberly-constructed world, Neo comes to the realisation that his body lives in a future ruled by these Artificial Intelligences. Within this dystopia, these machines have taken control of the whole planet and have enslaved the vast majority of human beings. The planet's resources have been depleted and a dense layer of smoke prevents these machines from using solar power. For this reason, human beings are kept alive so their human body can be used as a source of energy. Through a complex process, all human beings are born, live, and die in a type of capsule that keeps them constantly dreaming about the twentieth century. In these cocoons, they are fed a dense liquid. They are hooked to a vast network of tubes with many subcutaneous connections across their body which slowly turn them into a battery for these machines. The only thing left for humans to do is to dream. These dreams – i.e. the Matrix, this desert of the real – are generated and controlled by these Artificial Intelligences.

The Matrix is a science-fiction cyber-thriller but it has also a variety of subtextual religious meanings. The parallel with a subtextual Messiah is easy to make when Neo, like Jesus, is discovered to be the long-awaited Messiah who will save humans from these machines. He is killed towards the end of the movie to be resurrected afterwards as a "divine" creature. Ford (2000) also sees in this movie strong Eastern resonances, especially with the Indian school of Buddhism which asserts that the objective world we perceive to be real is only a product of our mind. The point here is that this movie can have different religious and philosophical meanings, and that there appears to be no limit to our interpretation of the story's rich subtexts. Indeed, I could have easily interpreted the taking of the red pill as the eating of the apple of knowledge in Genesis – and indeed, Neo gets kicked out of his paradise – the Matrix – to be sent into the real world – a place where humans have to hide to survive. However, the point of this chapter is that the taking of the red pill can also support the interpretation of a quick way to gain knowledge through technological means rather than through many years of ascetism/meditation.

In previous narratives with esoteric subtexts – especially those before the 1960s –, the person seeking secret knowledge has to go through a difficult path that often requires a lifelong learning process. Some high quality novels like *Steppenwolf* by Hermann Hesse and *L'oeuvre au Noir* by Marguerite Yourcenar reflect the lifelong difficulty that human beings have in seeking esoteric knowledge. The characters in these "old fashion" fictions are perceived as metaphorically walking – and often tiptoeing – across in one of those labyrinths that can easily be found in a continental church/cathedral. They try different ways, always making mistakes, to find one right path to the centre; the centre of knowledge. This takes years of research and reflection/meditation and is not easily gained; as if the harder it is to reach the center, the better the knowledge and the skills acquired while seeking it. In *The Matrix*, on the other hand, everything is gained through the simple ingestion of a pill.

This chapter argues that the perception of gaining secret knowledge has changed in consumer culture, and this has had a repercussion on how secret knowledge is approached in popular culture and in today's spiritualities. Neo discovers the knowledge/secret of the universe as quickly as it takes the pill to work. The shock of the reality upsets him and it takes a whole month for his body – a body he has never put in motion in reality – to move again; all this is with the help of technology. Also, through the use of computers, he gains some superpowers that he can use as a "super" Zen master in the Matrix.

This example from popular culture illustrates a recent tendency within western culture. Indeed, within consumer society, perennism can be seen as the simplification of western esotericism – that is, a philosophy and a practice involving a "secret knowledge"; it includes, for example, alchemy, hermeticism, Christian Kabbala, Paracelsianism, and a number of initiatic societies.

Esotericism

In numerous studies, the concept of esotericism – and also that of occultism and Gnosticism – is used in many different ways that confuse. Almost all esotericists, i.e. people practising esotericism, use the concept of esotericism as a label for their teachings. Riffard (1990) provides an interesting analysis of the word in its various interpretations by different groups. For example, Gnosticism called esotericism gnosis; for Pythagoreanism esotericism was synonymous with philosophy (*o.c.*: 97); esotericism was magic for the Iranian Mazdeism (*o.c.*: 113); in 1883 the word was consecrated for the public in a book by A.P. Sinnet, *Esoteric Buddhism*, but the term was then used to express the doctrine of the Theosophical Society (Riffard, 1990: 78-79). For Foster Bailey (1974: 10) from the Arcane school, esotericism is the secret knowledge found in the work of the founder of the Theosophical Society, Helena Petrovna Blavatsky. For other esotericists, such as René Guénon, Blavatsky is a charlatan and does not know anything about esotericism. The word esotericism has thus a diversity of denotations. It is also so often strongly valorised in a variety of esoteric groups that it has been appropriated by them to establish their credentials with their peers and their public.

Riffard (1990) argues that the most visible characteristic, the affirmation most often renewed among esotericists, is the cult of the secret. However, Faivre (1994) warns us of the danger of reducing esotericism – this multi-dimensional term – to the secrecy dimension. However, this approach will be refined in the next section on Simmel.

Within perennism, esoteric knowledge is no longer secret (Schlegel, 1995; Trevelyan, 1984) and even appears to have become a public commodity (York, 2001a & 2001b; Werbner, 1995). There is no more need to access "secret wisdom" in groups because the access for individuals is now facilitated thanks to the structure of consumer culture. Every spiritual technique – e.g. astrology, numerology, and occultist rituals – is now easy to find and to learn and there is no need to belong to any secret group. Steve Cranmer (1995: 4), on the Internet, even warns people wanting to become a member of an occultist group: "Don't count on having "secrets" revealed to you. Ninety-nine percent of them are already published, in some form, somewhere".

Secrecy, a key element of esotericism, has been opened up, and is now on the shelves of New Age bookshops, and even on the Internet. As Zygmunt Bauman (1998) notices, if transcendence was once the privilege of an aristocracy of culture such as mystics, ascetic monks, dervishes or occultist leaders, now this transcendence is in every individual's reach, is part of consumer culture, and is thus commodified.

This process of giving to the public "secret knowledge" started with the advent of modernity and with the birth of modern Spiritualism in 1848 when the Fox sisters discovered a way of communicating with the spirit of a dead person through mysterious raps and knocks. They began their career as spirit mediums through newspaper journalism and toured throughout America. Their popularity created an intense interest and controversy and was the starting point of the modern Spiritualist movement.

Contacts with entities from the other world are not a new phenomenon in the history of esotericism. Shamans experience a trance and speak with "astral" people; mediums let their body be possessed by a spiritual entity and become transmitters of the supernatural. Before Spiritualism, this was called nekyomancy, necromancy or divination by consultation with the dead. What really makes the difference with the appearance of modern Spiritualism, is that suddenly people no longer need psychic power or long training to communicate with the world of the spirit. No longer does an individual need to be a shaman and experience a trance to speak with astral "people" or be a medium and let their body be possessed by a spiritual entity. Everybody is now considered able to contact the spirit of the dead and there is no longer a need for the presence of an intermediary.

Léon Rivail (1804-1869), under the pseudonym of Alain Kardec, tried to unify and codify Spiritualism to make it a religion "tinted with sentimentalism and rationalism" (Faivre, 1992: 86). Having positivist beliefs, without being an orthodox positivist, he employed the scientific method of observation, comparison and evaluation to systemise Spiritualism. He was among the first – if not the first – to reintroduce the theory of reincarnation in the West since its condemnation in AD 533 by the Fathers of the Church, but he reintroduced it with the law of constant progress, i.e. blended with a significant spiritual borrowing of Darwinism.

After Kardec's work, the large family of Spiritualism divided into two main tendencies. One – often referred to as Spiritism – followed his work, e.g. the Brazilian Spiritist Federation created in 1874. The other refused his systemisation and turned to predecessors of the movement, like Swedenborg for example, to rationalise Spiritualism with a Christian faith.

Later, in 1875, the Theosophical Society, a movement moving away from modern Spiritualism, was nevertheless following the same ethos of offering the secret of the other world(s) without the service of an intermediary elite – such as Brahmans and the priests of Memphis, Eleusis and Orphism. One of the founders, Helena Petrovna Blavatsky synthesised a new eschatology which was based on evolutionism and the theory of reincarnation in her *magnum opus, The Secret Doctrine.* Blavatsky did not reject Darwinism but insisted that it had omitted the spiritual side of evolutionism in favour of materialism. Inspired by an evolutionist discourse, she adapted and westernised the concept of reincarnation by syncretising it with the concept of spiritual progress. In the East, reincarnation is not only progressive – i.e. allowing the possibility of a better embodiment in the next life – but can also be regressive. In the West, the cultural transaction between evolutionism and the theory of reincarnation allowed only for progressive reincarnation: progress on a symbolic spiritual ladder, until the final theomorphic stage. Reincarnation is not, in this sense, a fate from which humans may have to be liberated as it is in the East, but a factor of progress. Thus the theory of progressive reincarnation explains how utopia is attained: one day the whole of humankind will have developed its divine sparks and built a world similar to that of Adam and Eve before their fall. However, this time, according to the early members of the Theosophical Society, is still far away. Serious spiritual progress still needs to be achieved over thousand, maybe millions of years.

The Theosophical Society and Spiritualism were the two movements that not only democratised themselves, but also gave the opportunity for women to experience the esoteric culture. If previously esotericists had been mainly male and seldom had let women participate in their rituals – unless a woman was needed for sexual purpose – in modernity, the latter had the opportunity to express themselves religiously.

If the Theosophical Society was mainly based on westernised eastern philosophies, modern Occultism was strongly influenced by the Kabala. For example, Eliphas Lévi (1810-1875) and Papus (1865-1916) did not condemn scientific progress or modernity and even integrated science into their teaching against materialism. They planned to elucidate all the mysteries lying in the esoteric traditions and wanted to unveil all the secrets.

Lévi, the pseudonym of Alphonse-Louis Constant, created a movement to fight against materialism in France. He was also a romantic, a communist, and a one-time Catholic priest. Papus, the *nom de plume* of Gérard Encausse, was considered the "Balzac of Occultism" because he left two hundred and sixty titles. He was a physician and an initiate of numerous occult groups. He believed in the cure of the body through the treatment of the aura. Patients queued for hours in front of his consulting room. He even received a medal of honour from the *Assistance publique* of France. He was also the spiritual teacher of Nicholas II in St. Petersburg.

This movement attracted people of apparently diverse personalities who did not condemn scientific progress or modernity but who integrated science into their teachings against materialism. They planned to elucidate all the mysteries lying in the esoteric traditions and wanted to unveil all the secrets. Many new initiatory orders were created from this movement, e.g. the Golden Dawn by Samuel Mathers.

Occultism kept intact the concept of initiatory groups – contrary to Spiritualism and the Theosophical Society – but published many books in "clear" or non-cryptic language unveiling all the information that was formerly kept secret. So just as modern science attempted to explain the secrets of the empirical world using a logical method, Occultism attempted, by open scientific inquiry, to unlock the secrets of the non-empirical world – though with adaptations deemed suitable.

In this period of esotericism, as characterised by the birth of Spiritualism, the Theosophical Society and modern Occultism, it was no longer necessary to find hierophants to learn; it was no longer a spiritual dependency because "books" explained. In this, Riffard (1990) sees a vulgarisation of esotericism.

But through the years, we can posit that this process changed from the idea of sharing the "secret" doctrine into the ethos of simplifying it. As an example, I compare the book by the modern Occultist Papus (1994), *The Tarot of the Bohemians*, which, even if it supposedly answers the secret of Tarot Cards, is difficult to understand. In comparison to a kind of do-it-yourself-in-five-minutes-Tarot-cards-reading book or a computer program on the same cards that appeared in New Age shops, I see a profound difference of complexity. The former still involves serious work by the reader and proposes some notion of universal knowledge, and the latter is faster to grasp by focussing on easy and

Esoteric Knowledge(s) and Popular Culture

quick information about the cards, and without entering into any theoretical underpinnings. The tendency in modern esotericism was to reveal the secrets and to present purported universal knowledge: the tendency in what Riffard (1990) calls Esotericism Simplified – i.e. the period of esotericism that includes contemporary alternative spiritualties – is to simplify what was already revealed a century ago and encourage the practitioner to develop the knowledge of himself or herself. I want to point out that what I express here is a major tendency. Of course, there are spiritual actors who engage in very profound spiritual research – or in search of universal principles –, but what is emphasised is that the simplification of esotericism has given the opportunity for everyone to have access to this knowledge. The access is offered in a commercially prepared form: it is quicker and easier.

What does this imply for social actors involved in these spiritualities? What does it mean for a "secret knowledge" to be commodified? Jean Baudrillard, whom we have already worked on in Chapter 4, whose theories are sometimes seen as being more about science fiction than about sociology (Rojek and Turner, 1993), can nevertheless help to answer this question. But before addressing this issue, Georg Simmel (1991), a social theorist of another fin-de-siècle, can shed some light on the sociological notion of secrecy.

Simmel and Secrecy

The working assumption for this chapter is that from the Renaissance to the 1970s, esoteric knowledge was kept secret – to a certain extent – among a spiritual intelligentsia. But why? Inspired by my reading of Simmel, I first explore the notion of secrecy and, secondly, discover three ideal-types of answers to my question:

> Simmel defines the secret society as an interactional unit characterized in its totality by the fact that reciprocal relations among its members are governed by the protective function of secrecy. This central feature is established on a dual contingency: 1) members of the interactional unit are concerned with the protection of ideas, objects, activities, and/or sentiments to which they attach positive value (i.e., which are rewarding to them); 2) the members seek this protection by controlling the distribution of information about the valued elements (i.e., by creating and maintaining relevant conditions of ignorance in the external environment). (Hazelrigg, 1969: 324)

Simmel (1991: 41) writes that at one moment of history, at one geographical place, an idea that was manifested and commonly held can become a secret after a structural change; and *vice versa,* the secret can suddenly become revealed and be "open". Simmel (*o.c.*: 67) remarks that secret societies emerge everywhere as a correlate of despotism and of police control for protection against the violent pressure of central powers. Also, he continues (*o.c.*: 88), as a general rule, the proliferation of secret societies is the proof of the absence of public freedom and a reaction arising from the need for liberty.

In this perspective, Simmel (*o.c.*: 64) remarks that the ostensible finality of the secret is, before all, protection. But could something else be understood for esotericism? The secret can, in this case, be fathomed as a finality in itself. As Simmel explains (*o.c.*: 79), the substance of those secret societies is a secret doctrine, a theoretical knowledge; it is also mystical and religious. It is a knowledge that should not be spread among the "common" people – at least before the phase of "Esotericism Simplified". Initiated people, therefore, form a community to preserve the secret; a secret concealed in nature, visions, religions and in every place that is considered hierophantic.

But why would this knowledge be kept secret among a spiritual intelligentsia? Inspired by my reading of Simmel (1991), I find three ideal-types of answers:

1- For protection, as mentioned above. In this case, the secret is like a virus that is fighting to survive inside the body – i.e. the society. Initiates are selected and are trusted not to make public the existence of the group.

2- For power. The secret gives a sense of power for those maintaining it. Keeping a knowledge secret inflates the importance of this erudition, and this can give the holder social prestige. As already seen in our discussion about superheroes (see Chapter 5) but under a different light, Wedgwood's (1930: 139) writing on ornamentation, as inspired by Simmel's excursus (1991: 52-63), can help us understand the importance of having a secret. This is worth being printed again but with a slight addition:

> In every individual there are two conflicting impulses: the one to resemble his fellows; the other to be different from them. Human beings are gregarious but they are also individualists. While everyone wishes to remain within the community, every normal individual desires to be in some degree outstanding in that community. Membership of a secret society provides a happy issue from the impasse arising from these conflicting desires. The very possession of a secret, as Simmel has emphasized, gives social prestige.

The separation into a secret society can thus lead to an ego-valorisation. People isolating themselves, in this case, might want to feel that they are above "common" people (Simmel, 1991: 93).

3- For a pedagogical purpose. In this case the secret is a finality in itself as mentioned above. Knowing the doctrine is not always the goal esotericists wish to achieve, but the experience acquired through this search is the key to the gnosis.

Gurdjieff (1978: 240), an esotericist, describes meeting a "wise man" on one of his many trips. The man expressed his beliefs in these words:

> Understanding is the essence obtained from information intentionally learned and from all kinds of experiences personally experienced. For example, if my own beloved brother were to come to me here at this moment and urgently entreat me to give him merely a tenth part of my understanding, and if I myself wished with my whole being to do so, yet I could not, in spite of my most ardent desire, give him even the thousandth part of this understanding, as he has neither the knowledge nor the experience which I have quite accidentally acquired and lived through in my life. [...] It is a hundred times easier, as it is said in the Gospels, "for a camel to pass through the eye of a needle" than for anyone to give to another the understanding formed in him [*sic*] about anything whatsoever.

In this perspective, the knowledge of a secret does not hold all of the answers for the seeker. Also, at times, the doctrine is not meant to be secret abstract knowledge, but at the very most, the practical details of a ritual. In this case, it is not the "what" to know that is important, but the "how" to understand. This is what the term *disciplina arcani* suggests:

> [...] the fact that the mysteries of religion, the ultimate nature of reality, the hidden forces of cosmic order, and the hieroglyphs of the visible world do not lend themselves to immediate comprehension or to a didactic or univocal explanation, but must be the object of a progressive penetration at several levels by each seeker of knowledge. (Faivre, 1987: 159)

Within this perspective, the goal of esotericism is to pass successive stages of advancement towards mystical enlightenment or realisation. These initiates are not hiding the knowledge; rather they create clues and rites of passage for the neophytes to find and to overcome. Every time the latter succeed in a stage, they experience the knowledge and feel it more deeply; they know it corporeally. Therefore, a doctrine will be kept secret for people who want to find it, mainly to force them to gain the experience of this knowledge.[1] For example, Alchemists write

---

[1] How is the secret divulged to esotericists? How is the progressive penetration by the neophyte of the knowledge possible? I find three possibilities:

1. by oral tradition (learning with a "master"), e.g. Gurdjieff (1963: Chapter 2),
2. by the deciphering of some manuscripts (the "bibliophile" approach), e.g. Alchemic books (Cavendish, 1977), the Kabbalic deciphering of the Bible, and
3. by initiations (rituals) – i.e. "a body of rites and oral teaching whose purpose is to produce a decisive alteration in the religious and social status of the person to be initiated" (Eliade, 1958: x), e.g. spoken word, written word and "corporeal word".

in a jargon to describe their experiments and the products they are utilising. They are using symbols to describe the elements they are manipulating, e.g. the sun is the equivalent of gold because they are both yellow – Mars represents iron because both are symbols of war. Alchemy is a work of patience to develop the divine spark, a work of perseverance not only to work on nature, but to understand alchemical knowledge encoded in riddles that provide clues only if correctly resolved. For example, alchemy manuals suggest the use of vitriol in first experiments. Vitriol is presented in the literature (Cavendish, 1977: 177) as a chemical product but really means, by notarikon,[2] "Visita Interiora Terrae Rectificando Invenies Occultum Lapidem": "visit the interior of the earth and by purifying you will find the secret stone". If the neophytes do not decipher the clue, they will be hindered in their quest for knowledge. If they persevere and finally resolve the riddle, they will be enlightened and ready for the next step, and will progressively learn the secret of alchemy and develop their divine spark.

The analysis of the notion of secret is multi-layered – it can be that of a group or that of the universe (Faivre, 1999) – and is beyond the scope of this book. However, one of the many ways to find the secret of the universe is through the method of correspondence (Faivre, 1994; Pearson, 2000); that is, a process of establishing common denominators between signs and symbols in the hope of obtaining an illumination and/or superior knowledge. It is believed that real and symbolic correspondences exist throughout all parts of the universe, both visible and invisible. This homo-analogical principle considers that things that are similar exert an influence on one another by virtue of the correspondences that unite all visible and invisible things to one another. It is a kind of hermeneutics which searches for some divine signatures, whether in holy text or in nature.

Indeed, Baudelaire tried to express this in verses:

Correspondances[3]
La Nature est un temple où de vivants piliers
Laissent parfois sortir de confuses paroles;
L'homme y passe à travers des forêts de symboles
Qui l'observent avec des regards familiers.

---

[2] The reverse process of anagrammatising.
[3] **Correspondences**
Nature is a temple, where the living
Columns sometimes breathe confusing speech;
Man walks within these groves of symbols, each
Of which regards him as a kindred thing.

Comme de longs échos qui de loin se confondent
Dans une ténébreuse et profonde unité,
Vaste comme la nuit et comme la clarté,
Les parfums, les couleurs et les sons se répondent.

Il est des parfums frais comme des chairs d'enfants,
Doux comme les hautbois, verts comme les prairies,
– Et d'autres, corrompus, riches et triomphants,

Ayant l'expression des choses infinies,
Comme l'ambre, le musc, le benjoin et l'encens,
Qui chantent les transports de l'esprit et des sens.

The entire universe appears to be a huge theatre of mirrors in which every object hides a secret, in which everything is a sign that hides mystery. If esotericists view the world as a theatre full of signs to be deciphered, Baudrillard would argue that the world is a great Television screen – or an Imax theatre – full of signs, but these signs can never be deciphered because, for him, reality has disappeared for ever; it is now hyper-reality, the collapse of reality.[4] For Baudrillard (1995):

> The world is like a book. The secret of a book is always inscribed on a single page. The rest is nothing but gloss and repetition. The ultimate finesse is to make this page disappear once the book is complete. Hence no one will guess what it is about (always the perfect crime). Yet this page remains dispersed within the book, between the lines; the body remains dispersed throughout its scattered limbs, and one ought to be able to reconstitute it without the secret being lifted. This anagrammatic dispersion of things is essential to their symbolic absence, to the force of their illusion.

Esotericists appear to have a more positive approach than Baudrillard; for them it is possible to find this page. However, it could be argued that this page has become harder to find in consumer culture. The signs that previous esotericists were looking for no longer make

---

As the long echoes, shadowy, profound,
Heard from afar, blend in a unity,
Vast as the night, as sunlight's clarity,
So perfumes, colours, sounds may correspond.

Odours there are, fresh as a baby's skin,
Mellow as oboes, green as meadow grass,
– Others corrupted, rich, triumphant, full,

Having dimensions infinitely vast,
Frankincense, musk, ambergris, Benjamin,
Singing the senses' rapture, and the soul's.

(Translation by James McGowan, Oxford University Press, 1998)

[4] Esotericists (e.g. Ferguson's (1981) book cover) and Baudrillard tend to use the same metaphor to describe reality, that of the Moebius Strip.

reference to a secret knowledge in the consuming world but to other signs ad infinitum. I will be arguing in the following section that "esoteric knowledge" has merged with hyper-reality to create a "McDonald-ised Occult culture". In this culture, the notion of secrecy has radically changed. It might remain a support for protection, power, and for a pedagogical purpose, but in a totally different context; that of consumer culture.

Seeking a Hyper-Real "Secret Knowledge"

Two short case studies will help us to understand what it means to seek "esoteric knowledge" in hyper-reality.

Anne was a confirmed Atheist until her mother gave her a "New Age" book written by Ruth Montgomery. This book made sense to her and she began to seek to experience the different aspects of the religious and spiritual field. She first was introduced to Christianity by a born-again Christian, but decided to leave the group she joined. She continued exploring the religious market and decided to follow different "New Age" workshops. She tried many different practices, including regression, to discover who she was in her previous life. She said:

> I've tried to be regressed. Which didn't work on me. But then they say it can take many sessions before you sort of [experience something], and you need to feel comfortable with the person and whatever, which I never did. And at something like [AU] $120 a session you don't want to go to too many sessions before you know that something's happening.

She also went to a Buddhist monastery and was ready to become a Buddhist monk. She left this place because she perceived that the monks were not completely "authentic" at times; they were watching the *Star Trek* series on television too often. She admits that she was attracted by the "glamorous part" – i.e. the part which offers "mystical knowledge" – of the esoteric/New Age market and hoped to become enlightened. Although she has never had any mystical experience, she still hopes that one day the light might come to her.

Steve has performed rituals in occultist groups for years. Tensions occurred in those groups and some people wanted to gain more power. Steve felt that politics was taking too much time away from the ritual of magic. He is now involved in a networking form of neo-paganism and calls himself an urban shaman.

He criticizes strongly the idea of people obtaining a "universal knowledge". He said:

> It's not uncommon for a third degree witch – which is the highest thing in most witchcraft systems – to say that she can solve all your problems be-

cause she has access to universal knowledge. Absurdities like this are common.

He also makes a link between this "universal knowledge" and the ephemeral nature of certain groups:

People are in one group and they go to another group, another group, another group. It's very common. And there's lots of groups around too and everyone's claiming hidden knowledge and all this sort of rubbish.

Unlike Anne, Steve claims to have had many spiritual/mystical experiences such as shamanic trances, astral travelling, etc.

From these two examples, it can be seen that this kind of spiritual actor lives in a world of choice, which is part of the consumer society. In this world, the individual becomes his or her own authority; the modern/postmodern person in the west no longer tolerates being told what to believe and what to do. He or she is faced with an over-proliferation of "esoteric knowledge" which he or she researches and experiences. However, in this phase of "esotericism simplified" as we have seen above, all this knowledge is now so easily accessible and not controlled by some "intellectual of the esoteric", it could be argued that the majority of spiritual actors are faced with what could be called the McDonaldised[5] Occult Culture: that is, an arena of esoteric and occultist culture in consumer culture where anything goes. In such a culture, esoteric philosophies – such as Swendenborg, Guénonism, Christian Kabbala – are mixed with conspiracy theories, alien intelligences, and Jedi religion; for example the X-Files with Kabbalah (Winslade, 2000). In this arena, half-truths are classed as scholarly work.

The McDonaldisation of Occult Culture is a process defined by Koenig (2001) and its central quality is fragmentation of knowledge. The Internet – which he uses as a case study – appears to be a strong medium for this type of knowledge and could be argued to be an element of Techno-Magick.

Techno-magick is what articulates the channels of discourse that disseminate occult knowledge. Not only is technology caught up in the trope of magic, it becomes the medium through which this formerly hidden knowledge is now available to any individual with access to the internet. (Winslade, 2000: 96)

---

[5] Ritzer (2000) claims in his book to have related his analysis of modern society or McDonaldisation to Weber's bureaucratisation in terms of the rationalisation of society. He defines McDonaldisation as "the process by which the principles of the fast food restaurant are coming to dominate more and more sectors of American society as well as the world".

With Techno-magick,

> The knowledge is always fluid, disembodied and haunting, never fully lo-
> catable, accessible at many different possible nodes, and available to anyone
> who wishes to engage in practice of magic. (*o.c.*: 97)

Because of this fluidity – on the Internet more specifically, but also in everyday life – the gap between high culture and mass culture has never been so narrow. This allows the blending of "serious/high/philosophical" esoteric knowledge with more popular and commodified versions.

This reduction of facts to hallucinatory speculations leaves no room for the controlling influence of "truth", and results in an endlessly fragmented labyrinth of unlimited choices. The McDonaldised arena leaves only an aesthetic way of stimulation and navigation in order to find one's path. In this McDonaldised culture, esoteric knowledge appears to have become hyper-real. It is no longer connected to reality but to a consumer culture which mixes esoteric philosophies with popular culture such as *Star Wars*.

If it can be argued that this over-proliferation and commodification of "esoteric knowledge" together re-enchant western societies by making magic available for sale, it might, paradoxically, have a negative effect on over-consumers of this knowledge: that of leading to a *blasé* attitude and a feeling of disenchantment. Coming back to Simmel's (1997) work, but this time to his essay on "The Metropolis and Mental Life" it could be argued that over-seeking mystical pleasure and "esoteric knowledge" in this McDonaldised occult culture might make the seekers feel *blasé*, because this process

> agitates the nerves to their strongest reactivity for such a long time that they
> finally cease to react at all. [...] An incapacity thus emerges to react to new
> sensations with the appropriate energy.

For example, in Lewis' (2001) survey on Satanism, one of his respondents claims that participants tend to leave the movement after realising that it does not keep up with Hollywood stereotypes. As one respondent claims:

> I feel that some people stumble into Satanism thinking they will be able to
> do as they wish from powers given to them by the devil (Satan) and when
> they realize that there is actually thought and intelligence within, they feel
> bored. Most want to be able to curse and kill or hate for no reason. Those
> who stay are sound in mind and spirit, and have a very strong will for life, or
> anything they do in life.

Another example is that of a neo-pagan group from Australia that decided to end its activities on the Internet because of the ways their beliefs have been commercialised; they have only left a few web-pages to explain this situation.[6]

Although Drane's (2000: 156-157) comment is focused on Christian spirituality, it encompasses the spirituality under investigation and is telling of this process:

> Though pre-packages consumerist spiritualities (both Christian and others) may appear to work for a time, they will not ultimately quench the spiritual thirst of the human spirit any more than the non-stop consumption of food or household goods can meet the fundamental needs of those who are struggling to make sense of the personal emptiness that can be induced by a commercialized commodity culture. [...] One of the consequences of the McDonaldized culture in which this search is taking place is that, for the most part, people are less likely to be concerned about the discovery of universal spiritual truths than they are about following what can seem to be just the latest spiritual fads.

As in consumer society in general (Edwards, 2000: 39-40), and more specifically in this McDonaldised occult culture, the insatiability of limitless consumption of "esoteric knowledge" might be reached when the freedom of the market becomes the ultimate unfreedom, where nothing is ever enough. Indeed, the case might even been made that the purest form of religious experience, the essence of religion itself, is also tainted by this process. Having mystical experiences does not seem to exclude consumerist motives. As Daniel, one of my respondents, said:

> At around 20 I started developing an interest in various forms of yoga and I think in a lot of ways you definitely have to say I was a little bit compulsive, obsessive with it. I mean maybe I was too intense about it because I would do [...] for instance, exercises until I would get like a nose bleed sometimes. It was like you know striving almost too hard to achieve some goal, God knows what that was. I think they have a term for it these days: Spiritual Materialism. Every time you have a spiritual experience you get a little mark, you know, or a higher rank. I must admit I was very much like that.

What happens if a consumer of this McDonaldised Occult culture has a *blasé* attitude and becomes disenchanted? I am tempted to argue that we can expect four ideal-types of reactions to this culture.

Case 1– Seekers leave this "New Age" market and join a more mainstream group, or religion such a Christianity or Islam. For example, I encountered the case study of Joanne and read the account of Pastor

---

[6] Internet site, http://www.fortecity.com/victorian/russell/457/clan_raven_moon.html (22/02/2002)

Meyer[7] who were so dissatisfied with New Age and Neo-Paganism that they moved to the Pentecostal church. See Chapter 8 for more accounts of this case.

Case 2– They push their dissatisfaction even further by becoming atheist. In these two cases, people would be the most disenchanted with this culture.

Case 3– They can find a New Religious Movement and settle down; e.g. the Theosophical Society, the Anthroposophical Society, Spiritualism, etc. They may still consume spiritualities and not adhere to any article of faith, but there is a sense of following an acceptable authority such as a text of reference or the doctrine of a spiritual leader.

Case 4– They persevere on this "McDonaldised" path, but still have faith in one day discovering the truth and understanding the mystery of things by themselves only; this being the case of Anne and Steve (see above).

In these two last cases, and more specifically the last one, people would appear to have a calling. Max Weber (1970), in his essay on "Science as a Vocation", concludes that the quest for a scientific knowledge, in a society which undermines research and its workers, is a "Vocation"; that is, that people wanting to do an undervalued and undermined job must have a calling. It could also be said that the *blasé* actors seeking for a "secret knowledge" in consumer culture, and facing all the problems and constraints as underlined by Anne and Steve, can also be viewed as having a vocation.

We have just touched on the implication of having a culture that has been secret for centuries until being revealed progressively when entering Modernity and being then simplified and McDonaldised when being immersed in consumer culture. This move to consumer culture has had the effect of bringing popular culture to an almost equal footing with more traditional esoteric knowledges. This, I have argued, might develop a *blasé* attitude to many practitioners. However, with this move towards consumer culture and towards an "equalising" of popular culture with esoteric knowledge, more needs to be addressed in the light of consumer culture, especially that of the stasis of religion.

---

[7]   Internet site, http://www.harrypottermagic.org/big_deal_hp_2.htm (19/03/04).

CHAPTER 7

The Logic of Late Capitalism
and the Stasis of Religion

Introduction

True Happiness This Way Lies
And have you ever wanted something so badly
That it possessed your body & your soul
Through the night & through the day
Until you finally get it!
And then you realise that it wasn't what you wanted after all.
And then those self-same sickly little thoughts
Now go & attach themselves to something...
... or somebody...new!
And the whole goddam thing starts all over again.
Well, I've been crushing the symptom but I can't locate the cause.
Could God really be so cruel?
To give us feelings that could never be fulfilled. Baby!
[...]
Matt Johnson, from *Dusk* (1992) by The The (Sony Music Enter-
tainment, UK, excerpt)

These lyrics express our human condition within a society of
consumption; that faced with desire in a world of choice, we never get
satisfied; we always want more as there is no limit to our desires.
"Could God really be so cruel?". This was already foretold by Kurt
Weill in his pre-WW II "Alabama Song". In this story, a person is
looking for the next whisky bar, and for the next "little dollar". No
reason is given for this craving, but not fulfilling it might lead to death.
When the polyglot Ute Lemper gave a concert in Sydney in 2003, she
explained the meaning behind this song before performing it. The
message from Weill is that the best way to fulfil our desires, is, para-

doxically, to not to fulfil them, but simply to forget them – perhaps in a Buddhist fashion – or as Matt Johnson finishes his song "The only true freedom is freedom from the heart's desires & the only true happiness".

We saw in the previous chapter with the McDonaldisation of the occult culture how the mass consumption of religion might lead certain spiritual actors to a *blasé* attitude. In this culture, religion, science, philosophy and popular culture are all mixed together. This would promote an infinity of combinations from the social actor to create his or her subjective myth. However, if the spiritual actor is part of this consumerist ethos, would the desire to consume lead to a permanent state of insatiability as Matt Johnson sings for us above? When we realise that we are finally getting what we want and we realise that it was not what we wanted after all, "then those self-same sickly little thoughts now go & attach themselves to something ... or somebody ... new!".

Following this line of argumentation in the realm of religion/spirituality, it would mean that this process creates new religions/spiritualities at a fast process. But what if it is always a combination of the same elements *ad infinitum*? What would it mean if we are always attracted by something new which is only a (re)bricolage of various existing elements? What would this mean in our postmodern world in which everything has been invented, and all that is new is only what is being re-mixed? The current literature already argues for a stasis of culture, but what if we are in a stasis of religion as well? The work of Jameson below will provide a better light on these issues.

Jameson's Late Capitalism

But how is it possible in a mode of cultural expression that by definition is superficial, to say anything about deep structures?
(Question asked by Stephanson to Jameson (O'Kane, 1999)).

We cannot ignore the changes that postmodernism portends, especially those that have affected alternative forms of religions, such as New Age and Neo-Paganism. While there are different ways of touching on alternative religions and postmodernism, as seen in previous chapters, new light can emerge from the theories of Jameson, an American Marxist following the tradition of the Frankfurt School who has studied postmodern culture.

For the purpose of this chapter, I will mainly focus on Jameson's (1991) famous essay "Post-modernism or the cultural logic of late capitalism" and apply it to what has been discussed previously. This chapter will not discuss the epistemological critiques of Jameson's work – see for example O'Kane (1999) from a Marxist perspective and

Rendon (2001) from a non-Marxist perspective –, but will simply address the scope of its application to the field of religion.

In his study, Jameson follows Ernest Mandel's (1978) book *Late Capitalism*, and identifies three periods in the development of capitalism. These are 1– market capitalism which is characterised by the growth of industrial capital in largely national markets – from about 1700 to 1850; 2– monopoly capitalism in the age of imperialism which coincides with the period when European nation-states developed international markets, exploiting the raw materials and cheap labour of their colonial territories; and most recently – from the 1960s – 3– the phase of late capitalism, which is that of multinational corporations with global markets and mass consumption; that is, the world space of multinational capital.

As shown in Chapter 2, we live in a consumer society in which the arts and culture have been commodified and turned into a culture industry. This was analysed early on by the Frankfurt School and this process has been amplified in postmodernity. Markets have become global and are dominated by large multinational companies. This has lead to major changes in terms of our mainstream lifestyle which is now about consuming in a massive fashion.

Moving towards an analysis of culture in this phase of late capitalism, Jameson argues that previously modernist culture could be judged against certain dominant standards – e.g., the distinction between high culture and low culture –, and might even be oppositional or shocking, whereas postmodernist culture – a culture symptomatic of this phase of capitalism – is fully commodified and tends to be judged in terms of what gives instant pleasure and makes money. We are living in a culture of the simulacrum in which "the very memory of use value is effaced" (Jameson, 1991: 18).

> And no doubt the logic of the simulacrum, with its transformation of older realities into television [and other types of] images, does more than merely replicate the logic of late capitalism; it reinforces and intensifies it. (*o.c.*: 46)

This postmodern culture has to be understood as a cultural dominant; that is, "a conception which allows for the presence and coexistence of a range of very different, yet subordinate, features" (*o.c.*: 4). Indeed, for Jameson, not all cultural production today is postmodern. As he states:

> Postmodernist theory is one of those attempts: the effort to take the temperature of the age without instrument and in a situation in which we are not even sure there is so coherent a thing as an "age", or "zeitgeist" or "system" or "current situation" any longer. (*o.c.*: xi)

As part of this postmodernist culture is a fondness for pastiche. If previously, art movements had clear boundaries – as often explained in their manifestos addressing the new rules of art (e.g. cubism, fauvism and surrealism) – postmodern art and culture is a free-floating, crazy-quilt, collage of ideas or views; that is, a pastiche. It includes elements of opposites such as old and new; modern and traditional; high and low culture, etc (e.g. Warhol's *Campbell's Can Soup*). It denies regularity, logic, or symmetry; it glories in contradiction and confusion. Depth in culture is thus replaced by surface, or even by multiple surfaces; that is, what is often called intertextuality (Rosenau, 1992). Postmodern culture makes reference to all previous styles, messages and ideologies developed by modern culture without itself being a specific style, message or ideology. It mixes everything without creating anything new.

The buildings of Las Vegas and the Westin Bonaventure Hotel in the new Los Angeles downtown area are a case in point. The Bonaventure Hotel is disorienting and offers no sense of proportion in its spatial arrangements, as Modernist architecture should do. The buildings from Las Vegas tend to be a collage of ideas mixing themes such as Disney and invented history – e.g. Ancient Rome – in their architecture instead of focusing on one specific style. Jameson views this architectural style as being populist and as a critique of high modernist architecture which often disorients the fabric of the traditional city and its old neighbourhoods. This postmodern architecture has a popular success, however "purists" would regard them as "fake and tacky".

Nostalgia films from mass culture are another example. *American Graffiti* (Lucas) and *Chinatown* (Polanski), both movies representing an historical content, approach the past through stylistic connotation, conveying "pastness" by the glossy qualities of the image and fashion. Indeed, in 1973, *American Graffiti* attempted to recapture the atmosphere and stylistic specificities of Eisenhower's 1950s as did *Chinatown* for the 1930s. Pastiche does not set out to interpret the past or to judge it against some standard, but simply plays images off against each other to achieve its effects and with no clear reference to an external or "deeper" reality. More recent movies following this process that were not explored in Jameson's seminal work are *The Wedding Singer*, *Moulin Rouge* and *Shrek (1 & 2)*.

In the *Wedding Singer*, for example, the characters evolve in the USA of the 1980s and each of them embodies certain pop singers (e.g. Madonna and Michael Jackson) or television shows (e.g. Miami Vice) rather than the real life of the 1980s. The 1980s of this movie comes out more from MTV video clips and popular television shows than from a real account outside of a television screen. However, the movie works quite well and creates an atmosphere redolent of a simulacrum of the 1980s.

Jameson also questions whether postmodernism is also related to the end of the primacy of class-based politics as the result of an increased social pluralism. Postmodernist ideologues, as labelled by Jameson (1991: 319), claim that new social movements (women, gays, blacks, ecologists, regional autonomists, religions, etc.) arise in the void left by the disappearance of social classes. For Jameson, however, both the new social movements result from the global expansion of capitalism in its multinational stage. Even if he believes it is right to take part in non-class based social movements, his Marxist perspective would also insist that such alliances are generally not as durable as those organised around class.

According to Jameson, postmodern culture is thoroughly secularised, and this is contested by McClure (1995). McClure (1995) argues that we should think about American postmodern culture rather in terms of a resurgence of spiritual energies, discourses and commitments. The author even views in this a religious revival:

> In suggesting that many postmodern texts are shot through with and even shaped by spiritual concerns, I mean several things: that they make room in the worlds they project for magic, miracle, metaphysical systems of retribution and restoration; that they explore fundamental issues of conduct in ways that honor, interrogate, and revise religious categories and prescriptions; that their political analyses and prescriptions are intermittently but powerfully framed in terms of magical or religious conceptions of power. (*o.c.*: 143)

He uses as examples the Latin American works of "magical realism" and the Afro-American and Native American novels such as these from Toni Morrison, Michele Cliff and Louise Erdrich where he finds the untidy resurgence of magical and sacred themes. Contrary to Jameson's *a priori*, postmodern fictions appear to offer a support of expression of the human experience in religious ways and do not appear to reflect a secularised postmodern culture. Perhaps there are even greater links between postmodern culture and religion, such as through the practice of certain religious groups?

Perennism as Part of the Cultural Logic of Late Capitalism?

It has been demonstrated in previous chapters that perennism -that is, contemporary alternative spiritualities (see Chapter 2) – is part of the contemporary cycle of capitalism, and connections with corporate capitalism have also been alluded to (see Heelas, 1993; 1999). In this sense, it could easily be argued that perennism is part of the logic of late capitalism. The culture that it creates and that it appropriates/borrows is, as already seen in previous chapters, a commodity. But can we also argue that perennism is a religious pastiche?

In perennism, there is a strong detachment from systematized belief and practice and an extreme form of individualisation (Possamai, 2000a). Indeed, as developed above, perennists consume culture and turn indigenous culture(s), history and popular culture into a subjective myth, and each myth must "speak to one's perennist heart". Further, as seen in the previous chapter, this process is part of the McDonaldised Occult culture in which anything goes, in which religions and philosophies are mixed with popular culture.

This consumption could easily be seen as a pastiche in which contradiction and confusion are glorified. Indeed by constructing their subjective myth, there is an eclectic – if not kleptomaniac – process of selecting culture(s) and religions/spiritualities in a way that gives immediate pleasure; that which "speaks to the heart". In this process, it could be argued that this consumption *à la carte* plays cultural content off against each other – as already seen in the McDonaldisation of Occult culture – to achieve its "spiritual" effect and with no clear reference to an external or "deeper" reality.

Further, when Jameson writes about nostalgia films, it can easily be extended to "nostalgia religions". As seen in Chapter 2, perennists consume history without focussing their interest primarily on historic facts and data. In this consumption, they approach the past through a type of religious stylistic connotation which gives a feel-good sensation to the religious consumer. History is, in this sense, a source of inspiration to be selectively – more than accurately – drawn on. As seen previously, this practice has been heavily critiqued by anthropologists and historians because these actors avoid a scientifically constructed "reality". However, without taking these critiques away, this process can be viewed, according to Jameson, as a mainstream postmodern practice.

Moving away from Jameson's Marxist approach, we can argue that seeing perennism as a religious pastiche or as a spiritual market can call into question the sincerity and serious commitment of these practitioners. As Mulcock (2002: 170) observes, these practices of consumerisms and cultural borrowing might evoke the superficial materialism that would come to mind to many outsiders, but this should be viewed instead as a way of life, as part of the daily routines of these perennists, and I would argue, as a new spiritual way of being in this phase of late capitalism; that of being a religious individualist who locates authority in his or her inner self (Possamai, 2000a).

However, if it can easily be argued that the perennist cultural consumption is part of a pastiche – or part of a way of life –, there are nevertheless some criticisms to raise.

First, if these spiritualities are part of the logic of late capitalism, there are variations in their belonging; some are more involved in the logic of late capitalism than others. For example, Ezzy (2001) researched the commodification of witchcraft and, for heuristic purposes, used the term "Wicca" to refer to the older initiatory tradition of neo-paganism, and "commodified Witchcraft" to refer to the more recent popularized movement which is fully submerged in the logic of late capitalism. As he comments,

> Although there is a wide spectrum in between, I characterized commodified Witchcraft as Witchcraft in which the majority of exchanges are commodity exchanges. In contrast, Wicca is characterized by the exchange of both knowledge and goods as gifts, external to the market. These gifts are embedded in familial-like social relationships of mutual and moral obligations. In contrast, commodified Witchcraft involves the exchange of commodities embedded in social relationships that are dissolved by the exchange, with no ongoing obligations. (*o.c.*: 42)

Kulchyski (1997) confirms this approach in his study of aboriginal cultural production in the age of postmodernism by arguing that if commodification is the dominant logic in this late capitalist world, it has not achieved anything like the total hegemony of generalized commodity production. There also remain many viable sites for resistance, such as the practice "by marginal and dominated social groups of deploying cultural texts produced by or for the established order in the interest or with the effect of cultural resistance" (Kulchyski, 1997). These sites of resistance can also be found in the "Wicca" groups as defined above by Ezzy (2001) and in the "other" wing of New Age that is not involved in pro-capitalism, is counter-cultural to modernity, and refuses to be involved in capitalist mainstream, as described by Heelas (1993; 1996). Further, Introvigne (2001b) makes reference to a kind of Next-Age in Italy. In this country, the commercialisation of this spirituality would be so high that it is now in a period of crisis in which "New Agers" are moving away from the "New Age" appellation in the hope of not being equated with some kind of merchants in a temple.

Second, this consumption of products into a "pastiche" might have a logic underneath this search for "sensations". As explored in Chapter 3, it was discovered that even if all perennists consume history and popular culture for their subjective myth, they consume in a way which will apply to their eschatology. An Aquarian perennist – who believes in the coming of the Age of Aquarius – will consume culture in a way which supports an evolutionary ethos, even if paradoxically he or she consumes in a postmodern fashion –; a presentist perennist – the most postmodern of these sub-types (Possamai, 1999b) – will consume culture for his or her subjective myth with a focus on the present; whereas a neo-pagan will be more interested in consuming culture in a way which will render plausible his or her understanding of neo-pagan values and lifestyles; such as having a nature based religion, worshipping the Goddess and following rituals and ceremonies.

These sub-groups are ideal-types and there is, of course, some overlapping between these types; other types can also exist. For example, the Rainbow Warriors described by Buenfil (1991) may represent another type. These warriors mix beliefs in the coming of the Age of Aquarius with neo-pagan perspectives and focus more on a deep ecological spirituality. Their Age of Aquarius is the "ecotopia millennium". Is this a spirituality blending the ideal-types of Aquarians and neo-paganism? Or is it a new type of spirituality more focussed on ecology than any of the other types? Unfortunately, this question will be left unanswered. These ideal-types offer an understanding of three types of cultural consumption or types of "pastiches" – not based on the more usual factors of class, age, gender and ethnicity but based on the multiple realities of these actors consuming in accord with their eschatology. It should be noted that the current literature on the sociology of consumption rarely takes into account the religious factor, and this book is but one attempt at fulfilling this gap.

There are thus forms of resistance against the total hegemony of the cultural logic of late capitalism from within these alternative spiritualities. There is also a strong resistance – if not stronger – from outside of these spiritualities; e.g. Christian fundamentalist groups. This will be discussed in the next chapter. Before this, we still need to analyse an outcome of the spread of this cultural logic; that of the stasis of culture and religion.

The Stasis of Culture? The Stasis of Religion?

According to Jameson, everything in art and culture has already been invented; all one can do is to re-invent. Modernist art movements have pushed the boundaries of styles and rules so far that it appears impossible to create any new content.

> There is [a] sense in which the writers and artists of the present day will no longer be able to invent new styles and worlds – they've already been invented; only a limited number of combinations are possible; the most unique

ones have been thought of already. So the weight of the whole modernist aesthetic tradition – now dead – also "weights like a nightmare on the brains of the living," as Marx said in another context. (Jameson, 1983: 115)

The artist is no longer a "genius" attempting new original ideas. On the contrary he or she is more a facilitator mixing and re-mixing already invented styles and content. This trend is to be extended to culture at large as well. Culture within postmodernity cannot create anything new; the apparent novelty in culture is simply a strategy – e.g. "pastiche", "retro", "appropriation", "simulation", intertextuality" and "resurrectionism" from the culture industry to make quick profit. As Hassan (1999: 308) claims, "the stasis of culture within late capitalism has thus produced a culture which is bounded and predetermined by the immediate needs of the culture industries". By continuously rearranging, re-packaging, reviving, and reinventing culture, the culture industry produces an *effect* of "difference", "innovation" and "creativity". However, the appearance of actual innovation is really illusory and created by technological advances. For example, the superheroes from recent movies such as *X-Men 1 & 2, Spiderman 1 & 2, Daredevil, the Hulk, The League of Extraordinary Gentlemen* and *Hell Boy*, look less tacky thanks to the use of computer generated images. Even if they are more attractive to the young generation than the old Superman movies and Batman TV series, the content – even if more mature – does not have anything new. As Hassan (1999: 308) emphasises, the cultural content has remained the same:

> In this period of accelerated globalization the industrialized countries in particular are experiencing a cultural stasis due to hypercommodification stemming from the imperatives of accumulation, and of too many capitalists competing with each other within a rapidly diminishing spatial realm. "New" cultural forms do not now have time to develop "naturally" as they once did when outside (or at arms-length from) the logic of purely capitalist production, consumption and domination.

Hassan (*o.c.*: 308-309) uses the example of television and popular music and argues that there has been strong technological development (digital TV, CDs, DVDs...) but that in terms of cultural content everything is almost the same or highly derivative.

Following this account on culture in general, what can be said of religious creativity? According to Jameson, everything in art has already been invented; all that one can do is re-invent. This could be extended to all different spheres of culture in western society including that of popular culture. If we follow this line of argument, can we also argue the same for religion? Is it possible to claim that, in the field of religion, everything has already been created and that there is nothing new in terms of content since *circa* the 1960s?

The most recent and visible religious acts of creation are from the New Age and neo-paganism. However, these were created in the 1930s-1940s in Europe, that is, a long time before their popularity.

An investigation into the lineage of the idea of the Age of Aquarius and other notions identified with New Age Spirituality has showed (Possamai, 1999a) that the latter is not a product of the counter-culture of the sixties and of the franchise of a fast food church, but the result of intricate transactions in the nineteenth and early twentieth centuries among doctrines historically underground. Alice Bailey (1880-1949), a former member of the Theosophical Society, interpreted the Age of Aquarius as the upper rung of human spiritual evolution, and accelerated the prophetic message of Blavatsky (see Chapter 6) with the help of recent theories of astrology (as seen in Chapter 3). She wanted to prepare humankind for the New Age and founded the New Group World Servers to foster a coming world civilisation through union of people of goodwill. New Age Spirituality with a new international vision had taken shape by the 1930s, even if it became mainstream in the 1980s.

In regards to neo-paganism, T.M. Luhrmann (1994: 41-44) traces the roots of neo-paganism in the occultist Hermetic Order of the Golden Dawn, an initiatory society founded in 1887 (see Chapter 6). The Hermetic Order fragmented and one of the new groups, formed in 1922 by Dion Fortune,[1] was called the Society of the Inner Light. This society influenced new groups coming out of the Occultist stream, but they were not yet identifiably neo-pagan. Luhrmann (1994) calls the groups influenced by Dion Fortune, the Western Mysteries groups which see themselves as the continuation of the mystery traditions of the west, e.g. Eleusis, Mithraism, Druidism. According to Luhrmann, these groups demand far more intellectual engagement than witchcraft does. The practitioners of Western Mysteries are grouped in fraternities or lodges, tend to be Christian, and often work on cabbalistic principles. They appear to be a contemporary form of modern occultism.

Further fragmentations of occultism, from the 1940s, saw the emergence of exactly the sort of neo-paganism under investigation. Gerald Gardner, who had met Aleister Crowley – from two occultist groups: the Golden Dawn and the Ordo Templi Orientis –, published fictitious ethnographies of contemporary witches mainly in the late 1940s and the 1950s. He claimed to have been initiated and had revitalised witchcraft –

---

[1]   Her real name was Violet Mary Firth (1891-1946) and her motto was *Dio no fortuna*, "God, not Fortune" (Riffard, 1990: 878).

i.e. neo-paganism – in the western world. For Gardner, witches had ancient knowledge and powers handed down through generations. This invention of tradition was claimed to be a revival of ancient nature religions. Witchcraft was organised in covens run by women called "high priestesses" who presided over rites of initiation for new members of the coven. Gardner shifted the elitist ceremonial magic of the Golden Dawn to a more populist magic which could be performed by everyday-life people. He also reduced the Judeo-Christian flavour of the Golden Dawn and added neo-pagan ideas. Prior to Gardner there was no witch-craft as a religion (Hume, 1997).

Perhaps the last great period of religious creation was with the boom-ing of New Religious Movements in the 1960s-1970s, many of which re-assessed the application of a Christian worldview, and many others which westernised eastern religions and rediscovered esoteric move-ments created at the end of the nineteenth century such as Spiritualism, the Theosophical Movement and various modern Occult groups. We could argue that the latter movements were part of the early phase of the development of Modernity whereas new religious movements coincide with the end of Modernity; the last attempt for innovation. Lambert (1999) sees Modernity as a challenge to established religion and as a source of religious innovation, and proposes that we should understand this period of time as a new axial period of the same type of that of the sixth to fifth centuries BC which was the era of Pericles, Upanishads, Jain, Buddha, Confucius and Lao-Tze. In this period of Modernity, we would have seen a stimulating period which would account not only for religious decline, but also for revivals, mutations and inventions. One of the outcomes of the development of Modernity is to foster a view of the universe which, apart from some anti-modernist groups, is pluralistic, relativistic, fluctuating and part of a loose network-type organisation. This promotes individual choice which leads to any possibility we can imagine. Individualisation, as seen before with the work of Lipovetsky, can, in postmodernity, be considered as the main feature of the changes in the new value system, especially that of narcissism. Lambert sees innovation in this. While I agree with Lambert, I would claim that the innovation is of new religious activity – i.e. of subjective mythologising – the innovation is not in terms of content. I will argue below that with the birth of mass subjective mythology came the death of religious innovation in terms of content, or what can also be called religious stasis.

We have already explored some new forms of religion in this book that have been created and/or inspired by popular culture. Jediism is a case in point in which the stories from a series of movies give a support for a new religion. However, as seen in previous chapters, when the religion is applied to everyday life, the content is backed up with older religions. Popular culture, it can be argued, might be a form of support to religion but does not bring anything new to the content of a religion. Hyper-religion is a new phenomenon in western society because of its de-differentiated aspect – i.e. the mixing of popular culture and religion – and not new because of its content.

I am tempted to argue that the last act of religious creativity in terms of content is that of UFO religions. Movements such as the Church of Scientology and the Raëlien Movement have both alien beings from our planet in their content. While ufology is not frequently made mention of among members of the Church of Scientology, it has been a part of the Scientologist creed for a long time. Their cosmology involves the incarnation of some aliens as human beings on Earth; a process which is at the origin of our humanity. Some members of the church recount their past lives as involving space ships, robots and mysterious beings from other galaxies (Rothstein, 2003). The Raëlien Church promotes itself as an atheistic religion which claims that the human race is an "artificial" life form created by the Elohim; that is literally, those who came from the sky. However, even if these two groups were created in the 1950s and 1970s, there are some strong antecedents in the religious work of Emmanuel Swedenborg (1688-1772) and of H.P. Blavatsky who claimed that certain occult and spiritual leaders – i.e. ascended masters – dwelt on Venus. Further, these UFO religions could easily be compared to the Cargo Cults from the vast island world of Melanesia that first took place in 1917.[2]

Since postmodernity, the move towards the cultural logic of late capitalism, and the birth of alien religions in the 1950s, nothing new has been created in the religious field. We might even be experiencing a stasis of religion. For example, New Age has been called an old religion because it uses many of the old esoteric techniques such as astrology and the tarot cards. However, in terms of practices, it is original in the sense that all belief systems and techniques are individualised. For example, there is no longer a quest for universal knowledge as found in older esoteric groups but a quest for a knowledge of the self (Possamai, 2001b). Not withstanding this, in terms of content, there has not been anything new since the usage of astrology to foretell the coming of the Age of Aquarius in the 1930s-40s and the development of neo-pagan rituals in the 1950s-60s.

---

[2] For more information on UFO religions, see Partridge (2003).

Even if the mass individualisation of religion is a characteristic of the novelty of our current times, it can be observed that this process is, paradoxically, being standardised. Consuming religion/spirituality for oneself, a most individualistic act, is part of the logic of late capitalism. As Beckford (2003, 212-213) underscores, religious groups that offer entirely fresh self-identities such as "born again, "saved", "enlightened" or "clear" consist of

> an investment that will produce practical benefits in everyday life for individuals. In other words, involvement in these individualised forms of religion is not so much a flight or escape from the pressure to make lifestyle choices as an expression of the same kind of "standardised individuality". An analogy with restaurant will make this point clearer. A wide range of cuisine is on offer in late-modern societies, thereby increasing the choices facing customers. But many restaurants belong to transnational corporations; and their menus reflect hybridised and standardised notions of taste. In short, the appearance of diversity and choice masks underlying pressures towards standardisation. Individual customers are certainly free to exercise their choice but they can only choose from items on the menu. (Beckford, 2003: 213)

The point about the stasis of religion does not go against the religious vitality of our time period; even if it can be argued that this vitality can be standardised. The creativity in the use of technology such as computer and the Internet to express and support a religion is widely used and allows – as seen in Chapter 3 – individualised religions. Indeed, personal religious involvement such as in spirituality is strong, and this might be the reason why nothing new has been invented in terms of religious content since the counter-culture period of our history. It could be argued that there is a hybridised and standardised notion of religious/spiritual taste in this period of late capitalism. Indeed, this might be seen as a paradox. If we come back to Hassan's (1999) discussion about the stasis of culture, we find that no new cultural forms can develop "naturally" as they once did because they are part of the logic of purely capitalist production and consumption. Religion today might be argued to be part of this logic of purely capitalist consumption. Indeed, by the hyper-consumption of religion by the social actors that we have studied in this book, no new religious form has the time to develop "naturally" because of the way they are standardly individualised almost as soon as they are produced.

CHAPTER 8

Popular Culture and
Hypo-Consumer Religious Groups

Introduction

This Present Darkness by Frank Peretti, an Assemblies of God minister, is a supernatural thriller that topped the Evangelical Christian
Publishers Association charts in 1988 and 1989 with 370,000 copies,
reaching 1,122,000 prints at the beginning of the 1990s. It has been
described as a Christian Stephen King novel.

The story narrates a conspiracy about New Agers, humanist psychologists and Satanists plotting to rule the earth and overthrow Christianity. The demonic cohorts of the New Age permeate the educational
system, various associations and businesses, and financial powers which
prepare for the coming of the Antichrist. The only defence to such a
conspiracy is the Church in which the role of the pastor is of great
importance.

Demonic activities are hiding behind these New Age activities and
Christians must be ready to intercede with prayer and react with the
power of the cross. Within this spiritual warfare between good and evil,
a few Christians fight for the soul of a small town called Ashton. In this
fiction, Christian prayers are opposed to occult incantations.

This thriller expresses the trend of some religious groups in their
view of current popular culture. Popular culture would be dominated by
global corporations which allow for the spreading of Satanic sub-texts.
For example, the novel, movie and games from *Harry Potter* would be a
stepping-stone towards the wrong/dark side of religion; such as that of
occultism, witchcraft, and Satanism. We have seen in previous chapters
that popular culture is used by perennists for their subjective myths. In
this chapter, we observe groups that aim at preventing such a process;
believing that this form of (hyper) consumption leads to the dark side of
religion. These works of fiction are part of the culture industry and
cannot easily be controlled and policed at the production level by conservative groups. However, the policing work can be done at the con-

sumption level. Consumers can be warned of the danger of certain works of popular culture. This can be done by a call to total resistance to dangerous popular culture or by a re-evaluation of the same works in the light of one's faith. This policing can also be pro-active by re-appropriating and producing their own version of popular culture such as *This Present Darkness*, to promote, for example, a Christian message. There are also consumers who meta-resist this policing of popular culture and are still faithful to their monotheistic faith. These four types will be explored below.

Not only do some Christian authors re-appropriate popular genres and turn them into a Christian fiction for the pleasure of Christians and for evangelical purposes, but many Internet sites are promoting readings and Christian exegesis from current works of popular culture as well. For example, the site of Marcia Montenegro[1] is designed among other things to promote a Christian exegesis of popular culture. She is an ex-astrologer who has a sound knowledge of alternative spiritualities. Some of her attacks can be strong such as that against *Harry Potter*, Marylin Manson (see below), and softer, such as that against the *Star Wars* movies. Her critique of the Force is that it is a flow of energy that has opposites such as good and evil that are "wrongly" equal. In this world-view, the dynamic of opposing forces holds everything in harmony. Whereas the Force has a dark and light side, the Holy Spirit is for Christians good only, does not need to be balanced, and does not fit with the mythology of the Force. Montenegro sees in *Star Wars* a mythos that, if re-evaluated, can serve as a good platform for parents for a discussion about various philosophies with older children.

Sites discussing popular culture from a more conservative point of view are numerous and we might expect them to be read widely. Indeed, a survey conducted by Larsen (2004) discovers that congregations did not only use the Internet to strengthen the faith and spiritual growth of their members and to evangelise, but also that 21 percent of Internet users in America – about 19 to 20 million people – have used the Internet to seek spiritual and religious information.

However, before analysing this process, we need first to return to theories on postmodern culture and on fundamentalism(s) to understand the meaning these social actors give to their actions.

---

[1]   Internet site, http://cana.userworld.com/cana_contents.html (03/08/2004).

Fighting Psychological Pressure in Postmodern Culture

Melucci (1996) writes about our contemporary time as being multiple and discontinuous, for it entails the never-ending wandering from one set of experience to another: from one network to another, from the knowledge and habits of one social sphere to those of another, semantically and affectively very different. Due to this, uncertainty might have become a stable component of our new behavior since we cannot move from one context to another and draw on what we have already acquired elsewhere. Everything seems to be in a permanent state of flux.

> Change [...] is a goal we find desirable and towards which our search for the new and the different is directed. But at the same time, change poses a threat to our security and to our established and habitual rules. [...] Consequently, the paradox of choice creates a new kind of psychological pressure, confronting us with new problems. (Melucci, 1996: 45)

What is this new type of psychological pressure? If we work on a crude continuum which can illustrate the reaction of social actors to our contemporary social malaise, we find at one extreme a person who faces in their everyday life a constant existential anxiety? This person would be an ontologically insecure individual and would be characterized by an obsessive exaggeration of risks to personal existence, extreme introspection and moral vacuity. On the other hand of the spectrum we might find a person who experiences ontological security; that is, a sense of reliability of persons and things aided and abetted by the predictability of the apparently minor routines of day-to-day life. He or she is not troubled by, or may even be oblivious to, existential questions. He or she is unable to cope effectively with risk situations, personal tensions and anxiety, and is faced with a predictable routine. Only a micro part of the western population is close to these ideal-type extremes. The large part of the population is moving back and forth towards the left or right of this continuum depending on the life they are experiencing at a specific moment.

According to Bauman (1998), fundamentalist religions would offer a stronger sense of ontological security to their members than hyperconsumer religions. This does not mean that being involved in alternative spiritualities does not provide a sense of ontological security. The argument at hand is that these spiritualities, being hyper-consumerists, do not provide a clear threat in their belief system. Fundamentalist groups, on the other hand, even if they are still consumerist, are hypoconsumerist because of their focus on their clearer and more established message – e.g. as found in the Bible or the Koran. Within hypoconsumerist religions, there might nevertheless be many interpretations of one religious message, but these are still less than the many interpretations of many religious messages found in hyper-consumer religions. For fundamentalist groups, consumerism does not happen outside of their religion.

This form of consumption is simply due to the belief system of the group. Perennism is a relativist and syncretic spirituality/religion in which the believer would claim that all religions are different and that there are different and equal paths to be religious. On the other hand, fundamentalism(s) would be an absolutist and exclusivist religion in which the believer would claim that his/her religious system is absolutely and exclusively true and that no other religious systems can compete with the sole true way of life. There are, of course, many shades of grey between these two extremes and one should read Charlesworth's (1997) work on the diversity of revelations to discover the complexity behind this issue. However, for the purpose of this book, it is suffice to say that, because perennism is relativist and syncretic, its approach towards the many forms of religions is hyper-consumerist. This approach is also transferred to the consumption of popular culture in which anything can be consumed for this relativist belief system; whereas absolutist religious actors would (hypo) consume from within their religion only and would consume the type of popular culture that fits with their creed and/or that is recognized by a respected authority. As part of this hypo-consumption, we can also find actions of contra-consumption which aim at preventing the consumption of certain works of popular culture (see below). What is of importance in hypo-consumerist religions is that the standard of truth is based on objective authority and not on subjective interpretations as in hyper-consumerism. Involved in this practice, as we will see below, is a "battle" to define the parameters of acceptable cosmology and soteriology found in popular culture.

Monotheistic Fundamentalism(s)

So far, we have seen that popular culture and perennism are part of the logic of late capitalism. We have noticed some resistance from within these groups in the previous chapter, however, where the resistance to some forms of popular culture is stronger is among monotheistic fundamentalist groups. Their cultural negotiations with popular culture are aimed at what fits and does not fit with their belief system.

Defining what monotheistic fundamentalist groups are is a difficult task. They might accept the scientific and technological components of modernity and reject at the same time the cultural components of modernity/postmodernity such as secularism, pluralism, relativism, permissive morality and liberal individualism. Since traditions are always socially constructed and contested, they are not traditional in a sociological sense, but are committed to the restoration of what a group regards as "traditions" (Beckford, 2003: 134). The term "fundamentalism" is an imprecise term that includes an array of various religious movements. It is also a term used as a label applied by self-proclaimed "non-fundamentalists". This appellation can also be expanded outside of the religious field to include various ideological positions in different cultural and social movements such as economics, nationalism, Aboriginal politics, gender... (Schick *et al.*, 2004). Focusing on the religious field only, we can get more inspiration from Lawrence (1998) who writes about three large types of fundamentalisms. Within these three types, there are, of course, a multitude of sub-types.

The first broad type is Christian Literalism, which is a subspecies of the Evangelical movements which started in the USA in the 1920s. These Christian fundamentalist groups are combating "modernist" theology and secularist cultural trends. They were strongly represented in the US political life when the Moral Majority was formed in 1979. This political coalition of fundamentalists and of other conservatives was led by Jerry Falwell who used his large television ministry. These Christian groups successfully revived the anti-evolution crusade and supported anti-abortion movements. There are so many various subgroups within these fundamentalist groups that a new term has emerged to describe the most absolutist/exclusivist case: "fundagelism" (Sutherland, 2004). It is used to distance extreme conservative groups from evangelical groups. This term is a compound of "fundamentalist evangelism" and embraces people who believe in the future as foretold by the book of Revelation; i.e. the destruction of Babylon (Iraq) and the immanent mass conversion of the Jews.

The second broad type is Muslim Terrorism which encompasses a diversity of groups. They view the West as an enemy and tend to be active in terrorist acts. They attempt to re-islamise their society previously "lost" to globalisation. Greifenhagen (2004) also points out that not all forms of Islamic fundamentalisms are extreme. Some are moderate and aim at making their society more Islamic by focusing on nonviolent means such as education, preaching, publication... There are, of course, many other Islamic movements which attempt to re-islamise their society as well, but are not necessarily fundamentalist. These moderate groups tend to look at the past as a philosophical model and not as an everyday life way of living; they are not necessarily antiwestern, but are mainly interested in contesting their own political system – e.g. nepotism, corruption, poverty, etc. –; and they often want to mix Islam, modernity and democracy.

The third broad type is Jewish Political Activism. Even if the religious messianic Jew, Yigal Amir, killed Yitzak Rabin in 1995, this branch of fundamentalism tends to be more activist than terrorist. They aim to use the state as a way to legitimise its use of force. Israeli politics and religion are so profoundly interconnected that there is a multiplicity of political parties influenced by religious fundamentalist groups. They tend to work towards an Israel for Jews only, and one of its many sub groups is Orthodox Judaism; the branch of Judaism that adheres most strictly to the tenets of the religious law – Halakhah. See Kuikman (2004) for more information on various sub-groups such as the Gush Emmunim and the Luba Vitcher Chasidim.

Lawrence (1998) provides us with an enlightened typology of global fundamentalism and underlines clearly that these are countless hybrid forms of each brand. For the purpose of this book, I will use these groups as an extreme example of hypo-religious consumerism. I am, thus, not claiming that all hypo-consumerist religions are fundamentalist, but that fundamentalism – as constructed in the sociological literature – is a case in point of this type of religious consumption. Between hypo and hyper consumerist religions, they are of course various shades of grey, and I only intend by the construction of these two ideal-types to heuristically detail two extreme approaches to consumption within the field of religion.

It must be noted that the vast majority of the examples below are focused on Christian conservative cases as they are more abundant in the literature and the Internet sites explored for this book. If this research had been conducted in Hebrew and Arabic, rather then English only, the data collected would have been evidently different. For this reason, the results of this research tend to be Christian-centric with an open door on Islamic and Jewish faiths.

Resistance to Popular Culture

Not only is popular culture part of the logic of late capitalism – that is, that the production of culture is made for profit and for consuming masses – it is also part of a large edifice of social control aimed at the extension of capital. No matter what moral, ideology, religious message... ought to be carried in popular culture, the one that matters in mainstream western culture is the one that makes profit.

As Schiller (1996) explains, the key process with this neo-liberal teleology is on the one hand filtering the cultural works that will go ahead, and second selecting people who need to work in these cultural industries who will follow the corporate agenda. Even if there are thousands of independent writers, filmmakers, video producers, musicians and other cultural producers, the large majority of the cultural work is part of a culture industry and is controlled and managed by a small number of giant corporations. We can assume that the large majority of cultural works are then policed by corporations, and those that are not – for example fanzines and Internet sites – are aimed at a small public.

> What corporate domination of culture means is that those who get jobs in the varied cultural fields are subject, in different measure, to the commanding logic of corporate business. This logic [...] insists on the unquestioned priority of extracting the largest profit possible from the specific cultural product. It should provide as well, unless it interferes with profitability, ideological comfort and support to the prevailing order (Schiller, 1996: 8).

As a working assumption, I would like to put forward that the production of popular culture is first aimed at profit. It will only deal with religious matters if the work can sell. For example, *The Prince of Egypt* narrates the life of Moses until he saves the Jews from Egypt. The movie finishes on a Hollywood happy/selling ending just when they escape Egypt. The story does not deal with the real/not-selling ending about the punishment by God of the Jewish tribe and its lifetime wandering in the desert. Twenty-five years ago, Monty Python's *Life of Brian* could not be completed until former Beatle George Harrison stepped in to finance it after EMI Films withdrew, fearing it was too controversial. The predicted controversy was though to lead to a financial flop. There are of course exceptions. More recently, Mel Gibson himself financed *The Passion* so the movie could be used as a means of spreading the word among the unconverted. There are other low budget movies that mimic Hollywood, such as the *Omega Code* and *Left Behind: The Movie* which were well received among Christian groups. Both movies were well promoted among congregations and through the Internet (Clark, 2003: 34). As such, I am not denying that religious groups might have an impact on the filtering process of popular culture at the production level – however, when it comes to reaching the mainstream population, it is secondary to profit.

What is of more importance for this book is the filtering of popular culture at the consumption level. Even if many works of popular culture have been financed by religious groups and relate to specific faiths[2], this

---

[2] See for example the Internet site that is a guide to religious feature films, http://www.adherents.com/movies/ (05/03/2004).

chapter aims at focusing on works of popular culture that are perceived as taking the religious consumer away from a more established religion towards a religion of the self bordering on the dark side of religion – e.g. Satanism, occultism, New Age and witchcraft, etc.

It is not the intention of this book to detail all forms of censorship engaged by fundamentalist groups. For the purpose of this chapter, I will rather make reference to the criminalization of popular culture; a term defined by Ferrell (1998: 71) as a process that recasts popular culture activities and identities as criminal and defines the social effects of art, music and media as criminogenic. This does not simply involve the simple application of criminal laws. Rather, it implies a complex cultural process that occurs within the realm of media representation. These criminalization actions are more about controlling the presentation and perception of popular culture and controlling cultural representations.

Fundamentalist groups are involved in this process and aim to withdraw from the public space that which goes against their views on politics, gender, sexuality, and the family. Their role as "moral entrepreneurs" or "moral crusaders" is to promote their values, and criminalize other values. Sometimes, they see their values under a direct attack such as with the movies *Hail Mary* by Jean-Luc Godart and *The Last Temptation of Christ* by Martin Scorcese, Andres Serrano's photograph *Piss Christ,* Madonna's video clip *Like a Prayer* in which the figure of Christ receives physical comfort and pleasure, and Rushdie's *The Satanic Verses*.[3] Responses to these varied between demonstrations, bomb incidents, the burning of books and the issuing of death sentences. It is not my intention to detail all forms of censorships engaged by fundamentalist groups. What is of interest is the criminalization of popular culture that does not necessarily go specifically against mainstream religions, but are seen as being a cultural nest for Satanism and the occult; that is, the kind of popular culture that is being – or might in the future be – used by cultural consumers in their bricolage of subjective myth.

Of course, other factors of this resistance should be taken into account. All of the works of popular culture under study are from western culture, and this culture appears to the outsider[4] to be defined by junk food, clothing, leisure, rock music, television programmes, pop heroes, media celebrities… According to Ahmed (2004), the western media are

---

[3] Other interesting cases are that of Gibson's *The Passion of Christ,* which has been attacked by some Jewish groups and embraced by some Christian groups, and that of the movie *The Day After Tomorrow* which has caused some polemics among Christian fundamentalist groups because it wrongly narrates the apocalypse.

[4] If the concept of an outsider to globalised western still holds true today.

seen as hostile because Muslims in the media have no voice; the expressions of their cultural identity are often dismissed as fanaticism. For this reason, Islam tends to retreat from the media often with passionate expressions of faith and anger (*o.c.*: 257). There are clearly wider issues at stake in this analysis. We could think of specific religions and their power relation with the media – e.g. Islam and their belief of the media as the evil demon –, and how they are in affinity with western culture. Unfortunately, this is beyond the scope of this book.

This resistance is various and depends on the type of popular culture that is consumed. This section will only deal with some of the more mainstream and contemporary ones. These are *Pokemon, Digimon, The Lord of the Rings, Harry Potter, Dungeon & Dragons* and heavy metal music.

Pokemon was created in Japan and became popular around the world in 1996. Pokemon is short for "Pocket Monsters" and started as a cartoon involving little monsters that have to be caught by some popular characters. Many of these monsters are seen as "cute" whereas some others represent the forces of evil. The popularity of this story is part of a cultural industry, which has merged these cartoons with successful card and video games.

In 2001, Saudi Arabia banned Pokemon and anti-Pokemon campaigns are happening in Jordan, Egypt, Oman, Qatar and Dubai. Shaykh Yusuf al-Qaradawi, a widely listened to cleric close to the Fundamentalist Muslim Brotherhood, has recently joined the fight by issuing a fatwa on the 30th of December 2003. Some of the reasons he brings to his arguments are that Pokemon indirectly supports Darwin's theory of evolution and is thus contrary to the creationist view of the world; that the stories are constructed out of the authors' imaginations rather than from the surrounding "real" nature; that the stories always involved battles in which the stronger survives – another of Darwin's "dogma"; and that there are signs hidden in the series which are connected to the Zionists and Masons such as the "Hexa Star".[5] According to Tugend (2001), some Moslem officials claim that the word "Pokemon" means "I am a Jew" in Japanese, believing that this consumerist ploy is part of a Jewish-Zionist conspiracy to turn Arab children away from Islam.

Pokemon are also criticised by some Christian groups. Reading a few sources from the Internet[6], it becomes obvious that the perception that

---

[5]   See Internet site, http://www.cesnur.org/2004/pokemon_01.htm (27/02/2004).

[6]   Internet sites, http://sureword.faithweb.com/pokemon.html and
      http://www.godandscience.org/doctrine/pokemon.html and
      http://www.crossroad.to/text/responses/answerstopokemon.html (27/02/2004).

these creatures are teaching children about evolutionary thought and pagan/occult beliefs is strong. Pokemon is claimed to be the result of mystical/occult influences such as Buddhist Mysticism, Hinduism, meditation rituals, Egyptian Book of the Dead, Book of Tao, the Analects of Confucius, the Gita, the I Ching, and the Tibetan Book of the Dead. As one minister states:

> Recently I observed a group of children who were playing role-playing Pokemon. They were making evil faces and chanting their Pokemon character names over and over! One three year old was chasing another boy almost trance like in expression saying in a deep raspy voice: "bulbasore attack, bulbasore, bulbasore." They are meditating and projecting their spirit just like practioners of the occult.

Or from another Christian author:

> Children are being encouraged to tap into supernatural power instead of the power given by God.

Digimon, short for Digital Monsters, is a serialised cartoon close to the Pokemon "franchise" in which Digimons try to keep the world safe from "evil" Digimons. Although the fight between good versus evil might have an appeal to fundamentalists, references in some of the shows that wizards can be one's friend and that demons and devils can be innocent are of concern to moral entrepreneurs.[7]

Moving to another work of popular culture, we have seen previously that among other works of fiction, Tolkien's *Lord of the Rings* is being used as a source of inspiration for neo-pagans. However, accounts from some other religious actors are different. On a Christian forum[8], a Christian fundamentalist writes:

> Though [some] would have us believe that Tolkien's books contain simple allegories of good vs. evil, Tolkien portrays wizards and witches and wizardry as both good and evil. For example, a wizard named Gandalf is portrayed as a good person who convinces Bilbo Baggins in The Hobbit to take a journey to recover stolen treasure. The books depict the calling up of the dead to assist the living, which is plainly condemned in the Scriptures. Though not as overtly and sympathetically occultic as the Harry Potter series, Tolkien's fantasies are *unscriptural* and present a very dangerous message.

A response following this comment was:

> We may see some; yet we also see wizards using magic and spells. Now, this isn't christian symbolism, this is satanic symbolism. There is no way

---

[7] Internet site, http://www.breakthroughgaming.com/digi_poke.shtml (25/08/2004).

[8] Internet site, http://forums.christianity.com/html/p681045 (23/08/2004).

around this – a wizard in a movie is just as evil as a wizard in real life, for the Bible doesn't distinguish between the two. Furthermore, it's an oxymoron to have Gandalf the good, or Gandalf the white, because Gandalf is a wizard, and nothing "good" can be related to a wizard.

However, not all accounts from monotheistic believers are negative. According to Kilby (1974), the trilogy has indeed a religious meaning, but more specifically a Christian one. Even if Tolkien, himself a devout Christian, claimed to dislike allegories and to have written the story just to amuse himself, there is nevertheless a strong Christian sub-text. According to Kilby (1974), the whole story, even if not a sermon to be preached but a story to be enjoyed, must be given a strong spiritual reading of biblical inference.

From an Islamic perspective, an article posted on IslamOnline[9] acknowledges the credentials of Tolkien as a Roman Catholic (seen as cousins to Islam) Oxford Professor and warns against taking a "knee-jerk" reaction to Tolkien on the basis that it might advocate sorcery and magic (*Sehr*). Claiming that in the wrong hands, fantasy is capable of spreading *Kufr;* that is, a disbelief in Islamic monotheism, he does not recommend outright Tolkien's books and the new movie adaptation to Muslims. In his article, he is much less sympathetic to *Dungeons and Dragons* and *Harry Potter,* which he sees as emerging from the *Lord of the Rings.*

In the research for this book, it appears that *Harry Potter* has been more controversial than *Lord of the Rings.* Montenegro (2000) is a writer who was previously an astrologer and who converted to Christianity. Among other things she explores popular culture and comments on it from a Christian point of view with an elaborate view on "New Age", Witchcraft, etc. She makes a difference between fantasy novels that include magical elements and fantasy stories centred on the occult. Whereas Tolkien's story is just fantasy, Harry Potter would be a fantasy story using occultism. Harry Potter is argued to make reference to occult history and known practices – e.g. Nicolas Flamel and witch spells – and is not a work of pure imagination like the *Lord of the Rings.* As she states:

> There is a difference between fantasy and the occult. Fantasy can be used in a way that totally leaves out references to the occult. But this is not what happens in this book [Harry Potter]; instead fantasy feeds on the occult and is fuelled by it. Yes, this is just a story, but stories can teach and influence. Stories can present ideas and endorse worldviews. Does this book desensi-

---

[9] Internet site, http://www.islamonline.net/english/ArtCulture/2001/12/article12.shtml (23/08/2004).

tize children to the occult? What happens when they get older and encounter peers who practice magick, cast spells, and attempt spirit contact? These practices are becoming more popular, and are already widespread among adolescents.

As one Southern Baptist Theologian, James Parker, is quoted to have said (Anonymous, 2001):

Tolkien's wizard, Gandalf, is a kind of archangel sent from God who has special abilities to help people, [...] while the Potter wizard is a supernaturally empowered human being who performs magic that can be used for selfish or evil purposes.

Moving now to *Harry Potter* only, we can appreciate this quote:

Young readers can relate to Harry: he is the underdog hero who manages to triumph, and like so many children today, he longs for a family who will truly love him... Harry Potter contains powerful and valuable lessons about love, courage and the ultimate victory of good over evil. However, children who read the books will also be confronted with two distinctly non-Christian worldviews: occultism and secularism.[10]

Indeed, Harry Potter, a young English orphan who learns about witchcraft at a secret English school for young wizards, is an extremely popular character, and a likeable one. The plots reinforce the idea that evil is real and must be courageously opposed. It also teaches that human beings have to show courage, loyalty and a willingness to sacrifice oneself for others. Even if some Christian commentators, such as Neal (2001), might take a positive view of myth and fantasy and believe that some stories such as Harry Potter convey analogies to the story of Jesus, for many fundamentalist Christian groups the Harry Potter books are training manuals for the occult and have become the method of introduction of Wicca to the very young. Kemp (2002) makes reference to the reason why Canterbury Cathedral refused a "generous" contract from Warner Bros to film the story at its location. It can be summarised in the words of the spokesman for the Dean of Canterbury: "We did not think that books posed problems. But other people might take offence and so we had to say no". Indeed, it appears that imagery of witches and warlocks might upset some Christians. For example, Pastor Meyer[11] claims to have been a witch in the 1960s until being born-again as a Christian. He argues that the Eastern religions and "New Age" doctrine that are captivating congregations are basically a satanic set-up, and the Harry Potter stories are one set-up aimed at young Christians.

---

[10] Quoted from Bob Waliszewski by McManus on the Internet, http://www.marriage savers.org/Columns/C954.htm (27/02/2004).

[11] Internet site, http://www.harrypottermagic.org/big_deal_hp_2.htm 19/03/2004).

On a promotional Internet site for a video against *Harry Potter, Harry Potter: Witchcraft Repackaged. Making Evil Look Innocent*[12], we are told that sorcery is being introduced in all American public schools disguised as children's fantasy literature. The video/DVD is aimed at explaining to parents how to teach the children that spell-castings are forbidden territory. The site then lists a few accounts from children such as "I feel like I'm inside Harry's world. If I went to wizard school I'd study everything: spells, counterspells, and defence against the dark arts (Carolyn, age 10)" or "It would be great to be a wizard because you could control situations and things like teachers (Jeffrey, age 11)". It then concludes by stating: "Stop and Think: what will these children do when invited to visit an occult website, or even a local coven?"

These *Harry Potter* stories detail a fantasy world with wizards, mysterious and demonic creatures, and faeries where adults and children "are claimed to be led into imagined experiences that create memories, build new values, guide their thinking and mould their understanding of reality" (Kjos, 2000). In his Internet article, Berit Kjos (2000) compares the stories of Harry Potter and the Dungeons & Dragons (D&D) role playing games, and finds some strong connections between them.

Both *Harry Potter* and *D&D* are seen as creating a dangerous world of escapism in which the innocent can be drawn to occultism and neo-paganism. Indeed, playing a game dominated by magical incantation rather than prayers is seen as leading to a significant subtle impact on the player. As Schnoebelen (2001) states,

> How can a person, Christian or not, immerse themselves in a reality view so deeply and not have it impact the rest of their lives? This is difficult to imagine, especially considering the highly demonic and magical content of much of the game. As the saying goes, if you lie down with dogs, you get up with fleas.

Or, as found in a Christian forum[13]:

> The whole issue of Dungeons and Dragons is a very real one in and of itself. It is an attempt, an all too successful attempt in my opinion, to entrap young people into exploring the occult in the avenue of a game, and it can lead them to further investigate the occult.

In a Christian comic[14] aimed at children, a young teenage girl discovers the "dangers" of D&D, and feeling lost, she goes to a Christian

---

[12]   Internet site,

http://www.chick.com/catalog/videos/0127.asp (04/08/04).

[13]   Internet site, http://forums.christianity.com/html/p681045/ (23/08/2004).

[14]   Internet site, http://www.chick.com/reading/tracts/0046/0046_01.asp 02/03/2004).

meeting where a former witch speaks to the young congregation who tells them:

> Jesus sets us free from the bondage of witchcraft and gives us victory over all the power of the enemy (Satan). God's Word declares that you must *repent* of your sins and turn to Jesus Christ as your Saviour (Luke 13:5). Then according to Acts 19:19 you should gather up all your occult paraphernalia like your rock music, occult books, charms, Dungeons and Dragons material. Don't throw them away. *Burn Them!* We'll do that here tonight. We will also be praying for the deliverance of those who have allowed occult forces to control them.

Kjos (2000) blames the global market for the popularity of Harry Potter and *D&D* and states that "this process is reinforced by innumerable other occult images and suggestions created by an entertainment industry eager to please a global market – a worldwide base of potential customers that favour 'inclusive' and 'tolerant' pagan entertainment and turn their backs to Biblical values". As one *D&D* "apostate", now a recent convert to Christianity, claims:

> I have been through years of filling my mind with warfare, elves, magic, powerful swords and gloating demons, and having experienced the effects of this on my life. I heartily warn any Christian away from playing AD&D[15]. I do not mean to offend Christian role-players, but you do not realize how much AD&D is affecting your life, especially your thought life – I had no idea until my mind started being filled with scripture, what a devastating effect it had had on me.[16]

This process of resistance can also touch music. Heavy metal bands, such as Metallica and Megadeth have been accused of promoting Satanism or suicide. They have been charged in both civil and criminal cases and some of their concerts have been stopped by the police force or cancelled by the local government.

Indeed, some of this music, intentionally and unintentionally, does promote Satanist values. In a survey that Lewis (2001) developed and posted on the Internet, out of 140 Satanists who responded to his research, 2 (1%) alternated to this religion through music – one specifically mentioned Marilyn Manson who is a singer who often credits Aleister Crowley, Anton LaVey, Darwin and Freud as some of the major influences on his philosophy.[17] This is a very small percentage,

---

[15] Acronym for Advanced Dungeons & Dragons.

[16] Internet site, http://www.cs.rutgers.edu/pub/soc.religion.christian/faq/d&d (23/08/2004).

[17] People get involved in Satanism in various ways, however the majority tend to do it through reading (e.g. LaVey's *Satanic Bible)* and personal study.

but it happens. In a follow-up questionnaire, Lewis attempted to analyse pre-conceived ideas about Satanists, such as being involved in Role-Playing Games and having a deep appreciation for heavy metal music. From his data, there is some indication that there is indeed some interest in mainstream heavy metal music by Satanists, but hardly in more extreme forms such as "Satanic metal music". There was variable interest in Role-Playing Games.

Types of popular culture such as heavy metal music, *D&D* are seen as being used by "dabblers", i.e. young people who experiment with satanic material. Even if "dabbling" can be seen as innocent, this consumption is perceived by these conservative groups as turning them in the long term into the Satanists of the type that engage in child abuse and sacrifice.

Re-Evaluation of Popular Culture

We have seen above with the case of *Harry Potter* and the *Lord of the Rings* that some groups categorically oppose these stories, whereas others might find some inspiration; in this case they re-evaluate popular culture in the light of their faith. For example, on some Jewish accounts on the Internet we find that even if Harry Potter eschews Jewish values for some,[18] he can be for others[19] an ideal metaphor for what many Jewish teens encounter in their quest for religious growth. The previous section dealt with the most exclusivist case of resistance to global popular culture by the most fundamentalist and hypo-consumerist type of religious groups. This section, and the following two, deal with a less fundamentalist and hypo-consumerist approach.

We have explored in the introduction how an apostate of perennism critiques the notion of the force from the *Star Wars* mythos. However, her comments are not at all derogatory and she views many positive aspects as well. As she suggests to Christian parents:

The Star Wars movies, if seen by parents as well, can be a good platform for a discussion with older children of these various philosophies as compared to Scripture. The concept of the Force versus the personal nature of God; the dark/light dualism of the Force versus the absolute good and evil declared by God; and the emphasis on feelings in Star Wars versus the Biblical man-

---

[18] Internet sites, http://www.sdjewishjournal.com/stories/sept03_1.html (31/08/04) and http://www.aish.com/societywork/arts/Harry_Potter_and_the_War-Beween_Good-and_Evil (31/08/04).

[19] Internet sites, http://www.ou.org/ncsy/projects/5764/oct31-64/harry_potter-is_jewish.htm (31/08/04), http://www.aish.com/jewishissues/jewishsociety/Harrys-Magic.asp (31/08/04) and http://www.jewishjournal.com/home/preview.php?id=7724 (31/08/04).

date to use our minds and love God with our minds, are all productive areas for discussion, and a good way to teach your child to be discerning. The worldviews presented in Star Wars movies may be somewhat subtle, but such views exist in our culture and need to be understood and responded to.

The same author explores other facets of popular culture and on the controversial rock singer, Marylin Manson, she suggests a Christian response of outreach, not protest:

> Although we must be clear that what Manson espouses is wrong, we must also be careful not to self-righteously condemn him, nor should we turn our heads away when we see teens dressed in bizarre outfits. What kind of message does this send? It only seems to prove Manson right in what he says about Christians. This attitude is alienating. What good is it to reject those who already feel rejected, or alienate those who feel alienated?

> Instead, we should ask teens why they like Manson. Is it just the music or is it also the attitude and message Manson has? Be willing to address the issue of hypocrisy. There is hypocrisy in society and in the church. Why? Discuss this and listen. Be willing to admit some of what Manson says is true, because it is.

At *ChristianityToday.Com*[20], assistant editor, Todd Hertz, comments on *Buffy the Vampire Slayer* in an article titled: "Don't let your kids watch *Buffy the Vampire Slayer*: But you can tape it and watch after they go to bed". Although some of the developments and actions of the series do not fit perfectly well with Christianity, issues such as sex, magic and witchcraft are handled without glorification. The author recommends the reader to not let kids watch the show but that adults should nevertheless enjoy it. One of the reasons is that redemption seems to be a recurrent theme in the narrative; characters make mistakes and sin but pay consequences and change over time.

Certain books in the Christian literature explore popular culture to find what is of value to Christians without condemning the work. In *The Gospel Reloaded: Exploring Spirituality and Faith in the Matrix,* Seay and Garret (2003) argue that the first movie has a great value for Christians. Even if there are Gnostic and Buddhist sub-texts, characters like Neo, Morpheus, Trinity and Cypher are close to the Gospel. Other books (e.g. Johnston, 2002; Godawa, 2002; and Romanowski, 2001) explore popular culture in general and try to use it positively to illustrate sermons and outreach events.

---

[20] Internet site, http://www.christianitytoday.com/ct/2002/136/31.0.html (5/08/04).

Re-Appropriation of Popular Culture

As discovered, aspects of global popular culture are resisted or re-evaluated in light of specific religious faiths. A pro-active way to resist popular culture is to use successful formats of these works and offer content aimed at a specific faith. Many works of popular culture are created by Christians for Christians and potential re-born Christians. These are aimed at educating Christians and at proselytising. At this stage, these works of popular culture are not part of global popular culture, and their market – even if somewhat successful – is restricted.

This section mainly focuses on superheroes in comics and computer games, starting with *The Cardinal Adventures*. This Christian superhero produced by Sunday Comics Ministries, Inc., was created in 1990, has an undenominational faith in God and his ability to fly is a result of a God-ordained chemical accident – not a secular accident as seen in Chapter 5. The hero always tries to resort to non-violent action and bring to the story biblical messages. As described on its Internet site[21]:

> THE CARDINAL is a college student RICH BENTON, who attends Arbor City Christian College in university town, Arbor City. Born near rural Charleston, MO, he is the son of famed archaeologist Randolph Benton and wife Delores. Although he can fly, the Cardinal has no other superpowers and must rely on his faith in Jesus to get him through! Rich is not the most confident of heroes and often questions why God would choose him.

In one episode, the Cardinal catches a young thief who is armed with a pistol and is angry at the world. The boy asks: "What's wrong with anger? Everyone gets angry at sometime!". To which the Cardinal answers: "That's right, it's what you do with your anger that's right or wrong. Ephesians 4:26 says "In your anger do not sin. Do not let the sun go down while you are still angry…".

It is published as a free comics publication for numerous churches such as the Assembly of God, Baptist, Christian Reformed, Church of God, Evangelical Free, Free Methodist, Lutheran, Resurrection Life, United Church of Christ, Word of Life and other nondenominational churches. Churches, families and/or individuals use it as an evangelical tool.

There are other characters available, such as Major Victory[22] who is a toy company CEO and masked Christian superhero, and Armor

---

[21] Internet site, http://www.friendshipchurch.org/cardinal/cardinal.html (28/07/2004).
[22] Internet site, http://www.majorvictory.com/home.html (28/07/04).

Quest[23], a hero with the armor of God. Messiah[24] is simply the Christ as a Superhero.

Christian groups in the Anglo-Saxon world have used comics for many years, especially to illustrate both testaments. However, what is new, is that there is now a type of re-appropriation of what works in popular culture to carry Christian messages, such as the use of a Christian superhero. Contrary to Continental European and Japanese comics, the superhero genre dominates the Anglo-Saxon genre (Possamai, 2003). Even if some mainstream superheroes such as Superman and the Silver Surfer have biblical sub-narratives, there have not been yet superheroes with an explicit religious narrative.

On one Christian Internet site[25], the Web surfer is told that comics are an effective form of evangelism. Even if children and young people love comics, adults buy and read more of this para-literature than children. Many evangelists assume the power of conversion of popular culture and many testimonies on the site are listed to demonstrate this process. For example,

> I've been following Jesus Christ for about 9 years. A certain comic did have a significant part in my conversion. It was given to me when I was on work experience. The young trainee who I was instructed to pretty much follow around all day was a pretty fanatical Christian. He shared his testimony with me and set an example of how he stood up against bad morals, etc. and minor persecution in the workplace. I gave "Sledge" his nick-name (but) absolutely no indication that anything he said had affected me. But for some reason I kept the "Chick tract" that he gave me for years. The tract was "A Demon's Nightmare", and I don't know if it was the cool artwork or the spiritual significance, but I always held on to that tract. I ended up getting heavily influenced by evil heavy metal bands and fully believe that satan and his evil spirits tried to claim me and destroy my life. I was involved in crime and smoking dope. I completely lived in a fantasy world where I was fascinated by vampires and witchcraft. The desires were so deeply embedded inside me that I knew that I thought that this was my destiny [...] I didn't realize it was the deep carnal nature I was born with bringing me down. I'd never been to church. But anyhow I remember at some stage reading that tract and coming to the realization that I was on the wrong side of my Creator. I really repented and sought God. Sometime later God brought some other people in my life that led me to a Bible study and then to a youth ralley where I heard the Gospel preached. Somehow it all made sense that

---

[23] Internet site, http://communitycomics.com/cc_a2_dt_armorquest/index.html (28/07/04).

[24] Internet site, http://communitycomics.com/cc_a2_dt_messiah/index.html (28/07/04).

[25] Internet site, http://www.gospelcom.net/rox35media/ (29/07/04)

day, and I knew I had faith to commit my life to Jesus Christ. I'm a completely different person to the kid I was [...] I can actually look at myself in the mirror now.

Comics, in this context are used as tool of evangelisation. Not only is it important to bring people to Christ, but it is also more important to prevent people from what they view as witchcraft and Satanism. One such work of popular culture is the comic *Hairy Polarity and the Sinister Sorcery Satire*[26] created to warn people of the dangers of sorcery and witchcraft contained within the original series. The comics argues that *Harry Potter* is more than a fictional story and that witchcraft is real; the argument at heart is that wizards and witches think they are in control of themselves and of the world with their magic, but in fact demonic forces are deceiving them.

Moving to *Christian Games*, we can do some "screen shopping" at On-Line stores such as *Paper Street Games*[27] and *Breakthrough Gaming*[28] specialize in PC Games, Role Playing Games, Boardgames, of a Christian or non-controversial orientation. One PC game is *Exodus: Journey to the Promised Land* in which the player needs to help Moses solve the puzzle with 100 levels featuring mazes and other obstacles to faith. In *Captain Bible and the Dome of Darkness* – a Bible-based PC game – the Bible Corps send Captain Bible into the dome of Darkness, a city imprisoned by forces of deception. In this game, Captain Bible is armed with his computer Bible. Another game is *Eternal War: Shadows of Light* which is a type of Christian *Quake* – a popular first-person shooting game involving many nightmarish creatures. In *The Last Bible*, all but one of the Bibles in the village of Hampshire have been destroyed. Thomas must find it and has to overcome evil by using bible verses to save his soul.

Further, a few Role-Playing Games have been christianised. *Holy Lands*[29] is one of them and is advertised as such:

Holy Lands is also both historically – and biblically-based. Although there are elements of fantasy throughout, the game is set in medieval Europe – not a fantasy world. This allows the players to utilize history and the Bible (rather than countless expensive Sourcebooks) to embark on adventure while still exploring the imagination. The distinctions between Holy Lands and other role-playing games are its keys to excellence. First of all, Holy Lands stands alone because its fundamental ideal is based upon the Chris-

---

[26] Internet site, http://thetruthforyouth.com/special/hpcomic/index.htm (29/07/04).

[27] Internet site, http://www.paperstreetgames.com (23/08/2004).

[28] Internet site, http://www.breakthroughgaming.com/index.shtml (23/08/2004).

[29] Official Site, http://www.holylands.net/ (09/09/2004).

tian principle that morality is "black-and-white". Holy Lands has the bold-ness to distinguish virtue from evil! That is to say that the foundation for game-play is to make a clear distinction between good and evil because God, likewise, recognizes the distinction by knowing our hearts.

Another game is *Testament: Roleplaying in the Biblical Era,* which is based on the Dungeons and Dragons core rules.

Cases of re-appropriation of popular culture are, of course, not lim-ited to that of comics and games. As Tamney (2002) alerts us, some charismatic congregations use rock, heavy metal and blues – the type of music that more traditionalist groups have called demonic – with Chris-tian lyrics to make their church services more attractive to a certain type of the population.

Meta-Resistance to Popular Culture

Although the examples above are used to evangelise people, some Christians are interested in the "criminalised" popular culture for their own consumption. They are put in a position in which they would like to remain Christian but still consume. I refer to this process as meta-resistance; that is, resistance to the resistance process by monotheist groups.

For example, *ChristianGoth.Com*[30] is a virtual place for Christian Goths and other Christians. It does not aim at converting regular Goths to Christianity, but at proving to pastors and anyone else that not all Goths are Satanists or witches. This site even quotes Isaiah 9:2: "the people who walked in darkness have seen a great light; those who dwelt in the land of the shadow of death, upon them a light has shined". As one ChristianGoth claims:

> Once I received the Christ, I never lost my culture. They were certain things that had to go, certain things that didn't glorify God. But I still loved Sioux-sie and Bauhaus [popular Goth bands] along with my new found faith in the Lord Jesus. I found that contrary to popular "Christian" opinion, I could still wear lace and velvet (and, God forbid- eyeliner?).[31]

Some heavy/black metal bands view themselves as Christians. The popular group, *Demon Hunter*, has appeared on the soundtrack of the movie *Resident Evil 2* and straddles between being a "Christian band" or a group of Christians in a secular band. Furthermore, they are on a Christian recording contract.[32] Another band is *Mortification*, which is

---

[30]   Internet site, http://www.christiangoth.com (5/08/04)

[31]   Internet site, http://www.fehq.org/public/gothchrist.htm (23/08/2004).

[32]   Internet site, http://www.demonhunter/net (23/08/2004).

based in Australia.[33] This Christian style of music is sometimes referred to as "White Metal" or "Unblack Metal".

There are Christian role-playing support and advocacy groups such as the Christian Gamers Guild[34]. These groups promote Christian role playing groups without refusing science fiction and/or fantasy narratives. One person sums up quite well this tendency among Christian to use newest forms of popular culture for their faith:

> Christians have too long allowed non-Christians to dominate the imaginal world of role-playing, which was originally inspired by Christian men like J.R.R. Tolkien and C.S. Lewis, not to mention Dante, John Bunyan, and John Milton. I think it's time to be a creative force in role-playing and other forms of gaming for the true author of all creativity and imagination, Almighty God Himself.

In "meta-resistance", we find some elements of subjective mythologizing, but in this type, social actors are far from being involved in a hyper-religion. Even if they still (hypo-)consume popular culture for their construction of the self, they still have firm ground in a monotheistic meta-narrative.

Conclusion

Coming back to the findings covered in previous chapters, it could easily be argued that hyper-consumer religions tend to be relativist and syncretic and that hypo-consumer religions tend to be absolutist and exclusivist. Of course, depending on the different sub-types of these religions, there would be different positionings on this spectrum; however working on these two extremes can shed some light. Indeed, for any religion/spirituality that is relativist and syncretic the construction of subjective myths is built from many sources such as popular culture and various religious belief systems. Whereas, absolutist and exclusivist religions would not only put other religions on the side but would "criminalise" any text from popular culture which goes against their creed and/or support any other religions – especially neo-paganism and occultism. Of course, there are intermediary positions within these positions of "free consumption" and "criminalising" of popular culture, as we saw in the ideal-types of reaction by more conservative groups to global popular culture: resistance, re-evaluation, re-appropriation, and meta-resistance.

---

[33] Internet site, http://hem.passagen.se/bransell/mortification.html (23/08/2004).

[34] Internet site, http://www.geocities.com/TimesSquare/2964/ (23/08/2004).

CHAPTER 9

Conclusion

Following a long tradition of borrowing Greek myths to explain social and psychological issues, Galatea is perfect to symbolise the various social and cultural processes that have been investigated in this book. Galatea was an ivory statue that was so beautifully crafted that no woman came anywhere near it. It was the perfect simulacrum of a maiden that seemed to be alive, and only prevented from moving by modesty. Aphrodite brought her to life in response to the prayers of the sculptor, Pygmalion, who had fallen in love with the counterfeit creation.

The love of Pygmalion could be used as a metaphor to describe all perennists and other social actors involved in hyper-real religion; they have all fallen in love with various works of popular culture. These works have become alive in the production of their subjective myths and are being used as a strong support for their techno-spirituality. Popular culture has been used to inspire new religions/spirituality – e.g. the Church of All Worlds, the Church of Satan and Jediism. Even if many people use Jediism as a form of protest against the establishment, some of them are nevertheless clearly inspired by it for a renewed religion. Jediism is the perfect epitome of a hyper-real religion. From this analogy with this Greek myth, and carrying from Baudrillard's work on simulacra and simulation, it becomes more than tempting to be more ambitious and to even equate Galatea as the foundational myth of hyper-reality.

In 1999, I had a graphic short story published in *Tango* (No.3); an anthology of graphic love stories edited by Bernard Caleo that celebrate the City of Melbourne. I wrote the script and Greg Gates illustrated the story. The idea behind this story was to reverse the myth of Galatea. The narrative is set in the 1920s; here Galatea is a model for the sculptor Paul Montford. Although Galatea continues to love the sculptor after their failed relationship, Paul's only passion is his statue. With the progress of time the sculptor's frustration grows as his inspiration fades and his creation remains unfinished. In the meantime Galatea realises that Paul will never return her love, in desperation she joins an occultist group with the aim of making him love her for eternity. Following an occult ritual with great precision, she transmutes into the statue Paul had been creating. Galatea becomes the Water Nymph; an existing sculpture from Melbourne's Queen Victoria Gardens.[1]

In this mirrored-Galatea version, atheists and perennists have fallen out of love with monotheistic religions. One way to get them back is by turning these religions into a work of popular culture to promote their faith. We have seen how this works with the re-appropriation of popular culture process.

In this hyper-real testament, we have thus been exposed to two extreme forms of consumption: one that is hyper-consumerist and syncretic of a multitude of religions/spirituality and popular culture, another that is hypo-consumerist and absolutist in its faith and choice of popular culture. Hyper-consumer religions are in a type of free religious market in which the "seeker" works towards a subjective myth. Hypo-consumer religions are in a type of controlled religious market in which the believer follows an authority for his or her consumption. While perennism is a case in point of hyper-consumerism, fundamentalism(s) is one for hypo-consumerism. In between these two ideal-types of consumption, many other types of consumption that were just touched upon are to be found.

This hyper-real testament reflects contemporary practices in the religious field that cannot be left unstudied. These religious practices might become dominant in the near future; or perhaps, it is just a fashion created by the logic of late capitalism. Although, one should not forget that social actors have been consuming popular culture for their subjective myth since at least the 1960s.

Because of the involvement of religion in consumerism and its logic of late capitalism, it has been argued that, as for art and culture in general, nothing new in terms of content has been invented in religion. As we are experiencing the stasis of culture, we are also confronted by the stasis of religion. Even if hyper and hypo consumerist religions are a new phenomenon in tune with our postmodern world, they are not conducive to new religious creations. Modernity has created new religions which were attuned to their time – e.g. the Bahai'i faith and the Theosophical Society. Contrary to postmodernity, modernity was striving for progress and novelty and many new religions answered this call. Hyper-real religion is the most in-tune religion with postmodernity, and opinions on hyper-real religion will definitely be connected to opinions

---

[1]   I had no idea at the time of the writing that I would use this story for this book.

about postmodernity in general. On the one hand we can celebrate diversity and bricolage, on the other, we can mourn its depthlessness of culture. Whatever the opinion, hyper-real is here with us and is more likely to grow as it becomes more mainstream.

Postscript

At the time of proofreading the manuscript, I received an e-mail from the acting secretary of Matrixism letting me know of this newly emergent religion. It is based on the motion picture trilogy *The Matrix* and is claimed to have a history that goes back nearly one hundred years. Through an exchange of e-mails, I was told that Matrixism started at the end of July 2004, and since then, over three hundred people have joined this religion. Aside from people getting together, Matrixism takes place on the Internet.

Surfing their website at http://www.geocities.com/matrixism2069, we can discover a link with the Multidisciplinary Association for Psychedelic Studies and Matrixism's influence from Huxley's *Doors of Perception*. There are also parallels with the Baha'i Faith to validate the religious aspect of the trilogy.

This clearly relates to the possible expansion of hyper-real religion in our society.

References

AAP (2002), "Is Jedi Now a Religion?", *The Age*, August 27.

Agel, J. (1970), *The Making of Kubrick's 2001*, New York, Agel Publishing Company.

Agence France-Press (2002), "Jedi Census Ploy a Success", *The Australian IT*, August 28 2002.

Agger, B. (1991), "Critical Theory, Poststructuralism, Postmodernism: Their Sociological Relevance", *Annual Review of Sociology*, 17: 105-131.

Ahmed, A. (2004), *Postmodernism and Islam: Predicaments and Promise* (Revised Edition), London and New York, Routledge.

Andrae, T. (1987), "From Menace to Messiah: The History and Historicity of Superman", in D. Lazere (ed.), *American Media and Mass Culture: Left Perspectives*, Berkeley, University of California Press.

Anonymous (2001), "Baptists Find Morality in First 'Rings' Movie", *Register-Guard*, December 22. Internet site, http://www.cesnur.org/tolkien/008.htm (5/08/04).

Anonynous (2003), "Census Return of the Jedi", *BBC News*, 13 February. Internet site, http://news.bbc.co.uk/1/hi/uk/2757067.stm (7/03/2003).

Armitage, J. (2002), "State of Emergency: An Introduction", *Theory, Culture & Society*, 19 (4): 27-38.

Auerbach, N. (1995), *Our Vampires, Ourselves*, Chicago and London, University of Chicago Press.

Bailey, F. (1974), *Changing Esoteric Values*, New York, Lucis Publishing Company.

Bar-Haim, G. (1990), "Popular Culture and Ideological Discontents: A Theory", *Politics, Culture & Society*, 3 (3): 279-296.

Bastide, R. (1996), *Les problèmes de la vie mystique*, Paris, Quadrige/ Presses Universitaires de France.

Baudrillard, J. (1970), *La société de consommation*, Paris, Gallimard.

Baudrillard, J. (1979), *De la séduction*, Paris, Editions Galilée.

Baudrillard, J. (1983), *Simulacra and Simulations*, New York, Sémiotext(e).

Baudrillard, J. (1988), *Jean Baudrillard: Selected Writings*, Cambridge, Polity Press.

Baudrillard, J. (1995), *"The Perfect Crime"*. Internet site, http:// www. simulation.dk/articles/perfect_crime.htm (20/06/01).

Bauman, Z. (1994), "Modernity and the Holocaust", in *The Polity Reader in Social Theory*, Cambridge, Polity.

Bauman, Z. (1998), "Postmodern Religion?", in P. Heelas *et al.* (eds.), *Religion, Modernity and Postmodernity*, Oxford, Blackwell.

Beck, U. (1992), *The Risk Society: Towards Another Modernity*, London, Sage.

Beck, U. (2002), "The Terrorist Threat: World Risk Society Revisited", *Theory, Culture & Society*, 19 (4): 39-55.

Beckford, L. (2003), *Social Theory & Religion*, Cambridge, Cambridge University Press.

Beckford, J. and M. Levasseur (1986), "New Religious Movements in Western Europe", in Beckford J. (ed.), *New Religious Movements and Rapid Social Change*, Sage/Unesco: 29-54.

Bendle, M. (2002), "Militant Religion and Globalization", *Australian Religion Studies Review*, 15 (1): 5-10.

Berger, P. (1974), "Some Second Thoughts on Substantive versus Functional Definitions of Religion", *The Society for the Scientific Study of Religion*, 13: 125-133.

Beyer, P. (1991), "Privatization and the Public Influence of Religion in Global Society", in Mike Featherstone (ed.), *Global Culture. Nationalism, Globalization and Modernity. A Theory, Culture & Society* special issue, London: Sage: 373-395.

Bloch J. (1998), *New Spirituality, Self, and Belonging: How New Agers and Neo-Pagans Talk about Themselves*, Westport, Praeger.

Bodone, E. (1991), "Ethnography, Fiction, and the Meaning of the Past in Brittany", *American Ethnologist*, 10 (3): 518-545.

Bouma, G. and D. Lennon (2003), "Estimating the Extent of Religious and Spiritual Activity in Australia Using Time-Budget Data", *Journal for the Scientific Study of Religion* 42 (1): 107-112.

Bowman M. (1993), "Reinventing the Celts", *Religion*, (23): 147-156.

Brody, M. (1995), "Batman: Psychic Trauma and Its Solution", *Journal of Popular Culture*, 28 (4): 171-178.

Bruce S. (1996), *Religion in the Modern World, From Cathedrals to Cults*, Oxford, New York, Oxford University Press.

Buenfil, A. R. (1991), *Rainbow Nation Without Borders. Toward an Ecotopian Millennium*, Santa Fe, New Mexico, Bear & Company Publishing.

Campbell, B. (1978), "A Typology of Cults", *Sociological Analysis*, 39 (3): 228-240.

Campbell, C. (1978), "The Secret Religion of the Educated Classes", *Sociological Analysis*, 39 (2): 146-156.

Casanova, J. (1994), *Public Religions in the Modern World*, Chicago and London, University of Chicago Press.

Castoriadis, C. (1992), "The Retreat from Autonomy: Post-Modernism as Generalised Conformism", *Thesis Eleven*, (31): 14-25.

Cavendish, R. (1977), *The Black Arts*, London, Picador.

Chaney, D. (1996), *Lifestyles*, London, Routledge.

Charlesworth, M. (1997), *Religious Inventions: Four Essays*, Melbourne, Cambridge University Press.

Clark Schofield, L. (2003), *From Angels to Aliens: Teenagers, the Media, and the Supernatural*, New York, Oxford University Press.

Cohen, E., Ben-Yehuda Nachman and Aviad Janet (1987), "Recentering the World: the Quest for 'Elective' Centers in a Secularized Universe", *Sociological Review*, 35 (2): 320-346.

Cranmer, S. (1995), "The Golden Dawn FAQ". Internet site, http://www.bartol.udel.edu/~cranmer/cranmer_gdfaq.html (26/11/1995).

Crépin and Groensteen (ed.) (1999), *"On tue à chaque page"*. *La loi de 1949 sur les publications destinées à la jeunesse*, Bruxelles, Editions du Temps.

Crumlin, R. (1984), *The Blake Prize for Religious Art – the First 25 Years. A Survey*, Melbourne, Monash University Gallery.

Crumlin, R. (1998), *Beyond Belief: Modern Art and the Religious Imagination*, Melbourne, National Gallery of Victoria.

Cunningham C. & K. Egan (1996), *Christian Spirituality: Themes from the Tradition*, New Jersey, Paulist Press.

Cusack, C. (2003), "The Virgin Mary at Coogee: A Preliminary Investigation", *The Australian Religion Studies Review*, 16 (1): 116-129.

Cuthbert, D. and M. Grossman (1996), "Trading Places. Locating the Indigenous in the New Age", *Thamyris*, 3 (1): 18-36.

Daniels, L. (1991), *Marvel. Five Fabulous Decades of the World's Greatest Comics*, New York, Harry N. Abrams, Inc.

Davie, G. (1994), *Religion in Britain since 1945: Believing without Belonging*, Oxford, Blackwell.

Debord, G. (1995), *The Society of the Spectacle*, New York, Zone Books.

de Certeau, Michel (1988), *The Practice of Everyday Life*, Berkeley and Los Angeles, University of California Press.

DeMet, G. (2001), *"2001: A Space Odyssey* Internet Resource Archive: The Search for Meaning in *2001"*. Masters thesis, Internet site, http://www.palantir.net/2001/meanings.essay06.html (28/05/2001).

Dobbelaere, K. (2002), *Secularization: An Analysis at Three Levels*, Brussels, P.I.E.-Peter Lang.

Dobbelaere, K. and L. Voyé (1990), "From Pillar to Postmodernity: The Changing Situation of Religion in Belgium", *Sociological Analysis*, (51:S), S1-S13.

Dodson, M. (1994), "The Wentworth Lecture. The End in the Beginning: Re(de)fining Aboriginality", *Australian Aboriginal Studies*, 1: 2-13.

Drane, J. (2000), *The McDonaldization of the Church: Spirituality, Creativity, and the Future of the Church*, London, Darton, Longman and Todd Ltd.

Eco, U. (1976), "Le mythe de Superman", *Communications*, 24: 24-40.

Edwards, T. (2000), *Contradictions of Consumption: Concepts, Practices and Politics in Consumer Society*, Buckingham, Open University Press.

Eleta, P. (1997), "The Conquest of Magic over Public Space: Discovering the Face of Popular Magic in Contemporary Society", *Journal of Contemporary Religion*, 12 (1): 51-67.

Eliade, M. (1958), *Rites and Symbols of Initiation. The Mysteries of Birth and Rebirth*, New York, Harper & Row.

Eliade, Mircea (1962), *Méphistophélès et l'androgyne*, Paris, Gallimard.

Elliott, A. (2001), *Concept of the Self*, Cambridge, Polity Press.

Ellwood, T. (2004), "Invoking Buffy", in F. Horne (ed.), *Pop Goes the Witch: The Disinformation Guide to 21st Century Witchcraft*, New York, The Disinformation Company: 184-187.

Encel, S. (2002), "September 11 and Its Implications for Sociology", *Journal of Sociology*, 38 (3): 223-228.

Etzioni, A. (2002), "American Society in the Age of Terrorism", *The Communitarian Network*. Internet site, Http://www.gwu.edu/ ~ccps/ pop_ American-Society.html (18/09/2002).

Ezzy, D. (2001), "The Commodification of Witchcraft", *Australian Religious Studies Review*, 14 (1): 31-44.

Faivre, A. (1987), "Esoteriscim", in *The Encyclopaedia of Religion*, New York, Macmillan, 156-163.

Faivre, A. (1992), *L'ésotérisme*, Paris, Presses Universitaires de France.

Faivre, A. (1994), *Access to Western Esotericism*, New York, State University of New York Press.

Faivre, A. (1999), "The Notions of Concealment and Secrecy in Modern Esoteric Currents since the Renaissance (A Methodological Approach)", in E. Wolfson (ed.), *Rending the Veil: Concealment and Secrecy in the History of Religions*, New York, Seven Bridges Press: 155-176.

Featherstone M. (1991), *Consumer Culture & Postmodernism*, London, Sage.

Feingold, H. (1983), "How unique is the Holocaust?", in A. Grobman and D. Landes (eds.), *Genocide: Critical Issues of the Holocaust*, Los Angeles, The Simon Wiesanthal Center.

Ferguson, M. (1981), *Les enfants du Verseau: pour un nouveau paradigme*, Paris, Calman-Lévy.

Ferrell, J. (1998), "Criminalizing Popular Culture", in F. Bailey and D. Hale (eds.), *Popular Culture, Crime, and Justice*, Wadsworth Publishing Campany: 71-83.

Fiske, J. (1989), *Reading the Popular*, London, Routledge.

Ford, J.L. (2000), "Buddhism, Christianity, and *The Matrix*: The Dialectic of Myth-Making in Contemporary Cinema", *The Journal of Religion and Film*, 4 (2): 1-10

Gabilliet, J.P. (1994), "Cultural & Mythical Aspects of a Superhero: The Silver Surfer 1968-1970", *Journal of Popular Culture*, 28: 203-213.

Gallagher, A. (2000), "Weaving a Tangled Web? Pagan Ethics and Issues of History, 'Race' and Ethnicity in Pagan Identity", *Diskus*, 6, http://www.uni-marburg.de/religionswissenschaft/journal/diskus/gallagher.html.

Garret, W. R. (1975), "Maligned Mysticism: The Maledicted Career of Troeltsch's Third Type", *Sociological Analysis*, 36 (3): 205-223.

Gauchet, Marcel (1985), *Le désenchantement du monde. Une histoire politique de la religion*, Paris, Gallimard.

Giddens, A. (1991), *Modernity and Self-Identity: Self and Society and the Late Modern Age*, Cambridge, Polity Press.

Godawa, B. (2002), *Hollywood Worldviews: Watching Films with Wisdom and Discernement*, Downers Grove, Illinois, InterVarsity Press.

Guénon, R. (1958), *Symbolism of the Cross*, London, Luzac & Company.

Gurdjieff, G. (1978), *Meetings with Remarkable Men*, London, Picador Pan Books.

Greifenhagen, F. V. (2004), "Islamic Fundamentalism(s): More than a Pejorative Epithet?", in Schick, C., J. Jaffe & A. Watkinson (eds.), *Contesting Fundamentalisms*, Halifax, Nova Scotia, Fernwood Publishing: 63-75.

Grixti, J. (1994), "Consumed Identities: Heroic Fantasies and the Trivialisation of Selfhood", *Journal of Popular Culture*, 28: 207-228.

Hanegraaff, W. (1999), "New Age Spiritualities as Secular Religion", *Social Compass*, 46 (2): 145-160.

Hassan, R. (1999), "Globalization: Information Technology and Culture within the Space Economy of Late Capitalism", *Information, Communication & Society*, 2 (3): 300-317.

Harrow, J. (1994), "The Contemporary Neo-Pagan Revival", *Syzygy: Journal of Alternative Religion and Culture*, 3 (1/4).

Harvey, G. (2000), "Fantasy in the study of religions: paganism as observed end enhanced by Terry Pratchett", *DISKUS*, 6. http://www.uni-marburg.de/religionswissenschaft/journal/diskus.

Hazelrigg, L. (1969), "A Reexamination of Simmel's 'The Secret and the Secret Society': Nine Propositions", *Social Forces*, 47 (March): 323-330.

Henderson, L. D. (1987), "Editor's Statement: Mysticism and Occultism in Modern Art", *Art Journal*, 46 (1): 5-8.

Heelas, P. (1993), "The New Age in Cultural Context: The Premodern, the Modern and the Postmodern", *Religion*, 23: 103-116.

Heelas, P. (1996), *The New Age Movement*, Oxford, Blackwell.

Heelas, P. (1999), "Prosperity and the New Age Movement: The efficacy of spiritual econmics", in B. Wilson and J. Cresswell (eds.), *New Religious Movements: Challenge and Response*, London, Routledge: 51-78.

Heinlein, R. (1987)[1961], *Stranger in a Strange Land*, New York, Ace.

Himmelfarb, G. (1989), "Some Reflections on the New History", *American Historical Review*, 94 (3): 661-670.

Hill, M. (1992), "New Zealand's Cultic Milieu: Individualism and the Logic of Consumerism", in B. Wilson (ed.), *Religion: Contemporary Issues: The All Souls Seminars in the Sociology of Religion*, London, Bellow Publishing: 216-236.

Hodge, L. (1988), "New Bottles – Old Wine: The Persistence of the Heroic Figure in the Mythology of Television, Science Fiction and Fantasy", *Journal of Popular Culture*, 21 (4): 37-48.

Hoffmann, S. (2002), "Clash of Globalizations", *Foreign Affairs*, 81 (4): 104-115.

Holdstock, R. (1978), *Encyclopedia of Science Fiction*, London, Octopus Book.

Hugues, P., A. Black, J. Bellamy and P. Kaldor (2004), "Identity and Religion in Ccontemporary Australia", *Australian Religion Studies Review*, 17 (1): 53-58.

Hume, L. (1997), *Witchcraft and Paganism in Australia*, Melbourne, University of Melbourne Press.

Hume, L. (2000), "The Dreaming in Contemporary Aboriginal Australia", in Graham Harvey (ed.), *Indigenous Religions: A Companion*, London, Cassell: 125-138.

Introvigne, M. (1997), "Satanism Scares and Vampirism from the 18th Century to the Contemporary Anti-Cult Movement", Cesnur Center for Studies on New Religions. Internet site, http://www.cesnur.org/testi/vampires_wdc.htm (18/04/00).

Introvigne, M. (2001), "God, New Religious Movements and Buffy the Vampire Slayer: Massimo Introvigne's Templeton Lecture in Harvard". Internet site, http://www.cesnur.org/2001/buffy_marcho1.htm (14/03/01).

Introvigne, M. (2001b), "After the New Age: Is there a Next Age?", in M. Rothstein (ed.), *New Age Religion and Globalization*, Denmark, Aarhus University Press: 58-72.

Jameson, F. (1983), "Postmodernism and Consumer Culture", in H. Foster (ed.), *Postmodern Culture*, London, Pluto Press: 111-125.

Jameson, F. (1991), *Postmodernism or, the Cultural Logic of Late Capitalism*, Durham, Duke University Press.

Johnston, R. (2002), *Reel Spirituality: Theology and Film in Dialogue*, Grand Rapids, Baker.

Kadinsky, W. (1977), *Concerning the Spiritual in Art*, New York, Dover.

Kellehear, A. (1996), *Experiences Near Death. Beyond Medicine and Religion*, New York, Oxford, Oxford University Press.

Kemp, D. (2002), "*Harry Potter* and *The Lord of the Rings*: Contemporary Civil Religion and Some Christian Responses – Chasing Phantoms That Have Left Traces in Reality?". Paper presented at the 10th Annual Conference on

Contemporary and New Age Religions, Open Univeristy, Milton Keynes, 25 May 2002.

Kilby, C. (1974), "Mythic And Christian Elements in Tolkien", in John Warwick Montgomery (ed.) *Myth, Allegory and Gospel: An Interpretation of J.R.R. Tolkien/C.S. Lewis/G.K. Chesterton/Charles Williams*, Minneapolis, Bethany Fellowship: 119-143.

Kepel, G. (1994), *The Revenge of God. The Resurgence of Islam, Christianity and Judaism in the Modern World*, Pennsylvania State University Press.

Keyworth, G. (2004), "Werewolf Cults, Occult Lycanthropy and the Contemporary Werewolf Subculture", *Khthónios: A Journal for the Study of Religion*, 1 (2): 44-57.

Kjos, B. (2000), "*Harry Potter* and *D&D* – Like Two Peas in a Pod?" Internet site, http://www.crossraod.to/text/articles/D&D&Harry.htm (02/03/2004).

Koenig, P. (2001), "The Internet as Illustrating the McDonaldisation of Occult Culture", Cesnur. Internet site, http://www.cesnur.org/2001/london2001/koenig.htm (30/04/01).

Kozlovic, A. (2003), "Sacred Subtexts and Popular Film: A Brief Survey of Four Categories of Hidden Religious Figurations", *Journal of Contemporary Religion*, 18 (3): 317-334.

Kuikman, J. (2004), "Jewish Fundamentalisms and a Critical Politics of Identity" The Makings of a Post-Zionist Discourse', in Schick, C., J. Jaffe & A. Watkinson eds. (2004), *Contesting Fundamentalisms*, Halifax, Nova Scotia, Fernwood Publishing: 48-62.

Kulchyski, P. (1997), "From Appropriation to Subversion: Aboriginal Cultural Production in the Age of Postmodernism", *The American Indian Quarterly*, 21 (4).

Lambert, Y. (1999), "Religion in Modernity as a New Axial Age: Secularization or New Religious Forms?", *Sociology of Religion*, 60 (3): 303-333.

Langer, B. (1996), "The Consuming Self", in A. Kellehear (ed.), *Social Self, Global Culture: An Introduction to Sociological Ideas*, Melbourne, Oxford University Press: 57-68.

Langer, B. (2004), "The Business of Branded Enchantment: Ambivalence and Disjuncture in the Global Children's Culture Industry", *Journal of Consumer Culture* 4 (2): 251-277.

LaVey, A. (1972), *The Satanic Rituals*, New York, Avon.

Larsen, E. (2004), *Wired Churches, Wired Temples: Taking Congregations and Missions into Cyberspace*, Washington, Pew Internet & American Life Project, Internet site, http://www.pewinternet.org/ (04/08/04).

Lawrence, B. (1998), "From Fundamentalism to Fundamentalisms: A Religious Ideology in Multiple Forms", in P. Heelas (ed.), *Religion, Modernity and Postmodernity*, Oxford, Blackwell: 88-101.

Lee, R. (2003), "The Re-enchantment of the Self: Western Spirituality, Asian Materialism", *Journal of Contemporary Religion*, 18 (3): 351-367.

Le Cour, P. (1995), *L'ère du Verseau. le secret du Zodiaque et le proche avenir de l'humanité*, Paris, Editions Dervy.

Lewis, J., J.G. Milton *et al.* (1992), *Perspectives on the New Age*, New York, State University of New York Press.

Lewis, J. (2001), "Who Serves Satan? A Demographic and Ideological Profile", *Marburg Journal of Religion*, 6 (2). Internet site, http://www.uni-marburg. de/religionswissenschaft/journal/mjr/lewis2.html

Lipovetsky, G. (1993), *L'ère du vide. Essais sur l'individualisme contemporain*, Paris, Gallimard, collection folio essais.

Lipovetsky, G. (1987), *L'empire de l'éphémère. La mode et son destin dans les sociétés modernes*, Paris, Gallimard, collection folio essais.

Lowney, K. (1995), "Teenage Satanism as Oppositional Youth Subculture", *Journal of Contemporary Ethnography*, 23: 453-484.

Luckmann, T. (1967), *The Invisible Religion: The Problems of Religion in Modern Society*, New York, Macmillan.

Luhrmann, T. (1994), *Persuasions of the Witch's Craft. Ritual Magic in Contemporary England*, London, Picador.

Lyon, D. (2000), *Jesus in Disneyland: Religion in Postmodern Times*, Cambridge, Polity Press.

Lyotard, J.F. (1979), *La Condition postmoderne*, Paris, Les Editions de Minuit.

McAllister, M. (1990), "Cultural Argument and Organizational Constraint in the Comic Book Industry", *Journal of Communication*, 40 (1): 55-71.

McClure, L. (1995), "Postmodern/Post-Secular: Contemporary Fiction and Spirituality", *Modern Fiction Studies*, 41 (1): 141-163.

Maffesoli, M. (1996), *La contemplation du monde. Figures de style communautaire*, France, Grasset & Fasquelles.

Malhotra, A.K. (2001), *An Introduction to Yoga Philosophy: An annotated Translation of the Yoga Sutras*, Aldershot, Ashgate.

Mandel, E. (1978), *Late Capitalism*, London, Verso.

Marcus, J. (1996), "New Age Consciousness and Aboriginal Culture. Primitive Dreaming in Common Places", *Thamyris*, 3 (1): 37-54.

Marcus, J. (1998), "The Journey out to the Centre. The Cultural Appropriation of Ayers Rock", *Kunapipi*, 10 (1&2): 254-275.

Markham, A. (1998), *Life Online: Researching Real Experience in Virtual Space*, Walnut Creek, CA, AltaMira Press.

Marler, P. and C. Hadaway (2002), "'Being Religious' or 'Being Spiritual' in America: A Zero-Sum Proposition?" *Journal for the Scientific Study of Religion*, 4 (2): 289-300.

McDonald, K. (2002), "From S11 to September 11- Implications for Sociology", *Journal of Sociology*, 38 (3): 229-236.

McPhillips, K. and M. Franzman (2000), "Xena: Warrior Princess: Re-Imagining The Religious Cosmos", *Whoosh*, 44, Internet site, http://www.whoosh.org/issue44/mcphillips1.html (7/06/04).

Mejido, M. (2002), "The Illusion of Neutrality: Reflections on the Term 'Popular Religion'", *Social Compass*, 49 (2): 295-311.

Melucci, A. (1996), *The Playing Self: Person and Meaning in the Planetary Society*, Cambridge, Cambridge University Press.

Miller, T. (ed.) (1995), *America's Alternative Religions*, New York, State University of New York Press.

Mondello S. (1976), "Spider-Man: Superhero in the Liberal Tradition", *Journal of Popular Culture*, 10: 232-238.

Montenegro, M. (2000), "Harry Potter, Sorcery and Fantasy", *CANA: Chrisitan Answers for the New Age*, Internet site, http://cana.userworld.com/cana_harrypotter.html (03/08/04).

Mulcock, J. (2001a), "(Re)discovering Our Indigenous Selves: The Nostalgic Appeal of Native Americans and Other Generic Indigenes", *Australian Religion Studies Review*, 14 (1): 45-64.

Mulcock, J. (2001b), "Ethnography in Awkward Spaces: An Anthropology of Cultural Borrowing", *Practicing Anthropology*, 23 (1): 38-42.

Mulcock, J. (2002), "Creativity and Politics in the Cultural Supermarket: Synthesizing Indigenous Identities for the R/evolution of Spirit", *Continuum: Journal of Media & Cultural Studies*, 15 (2): 169-185.

Neal, C. (2001), *What's a Chrisitan to Do with Harry Potter?*, Colorado Springs, WaterBrook Press.

Nelson, G. K. (1987), *Cults, New Religions and Religious Creativity*, London, Routledge and Kegan Paul.

Neuenfeldt, K. (1998), "The Quest for a 'Magical Island': The Convergence of the Didjeridu, Aboriginal Culture, Healing and Cultural Politics in New Age Discourse", *Social Analysis*, 42 (2): 73-102.

O'Kane, J. (1999), "Contradictions, Overdetermination, and Dialectical Surfaces", *Socialist Review*, 27 (3-4): 107-146.

Ory, P. (1999), "La désaméricanisation de la bande-dessinée (1945-1950)", in Crépin and Groensteen (eds.), *"On tue à chaque page" La loi de 1949 sur les publications destinées à la jeunesse*, Bruxelles, Editions du Temps: 71-86.

Papus (1994), *The Tarot of the Bohemians*, London, Studio Editions.

Parker, C. (1998), "Modern Popular Religion: A Complex Object of Study for Sociology", *International Sociology*, 13 (2): 195-212.

Parkins, W. (2001), "Oprah Winfey's Change Your Life TV and the Spiritual Everyday", *Continuum: Journal of Media & Cultural Studies*, (15)2: 145-157.

Partridge, C. (ed.) (2003), *UFO Religions*, London, Routledge.

Pearson, J. (2000), "Wicca, Esotericism and Living Nature: Assessing Wicca as Nature Religion", *The Virtual Pomegranate*. Internet site, http://www. inter-chg.ubc.ca/fmuntean/POM14a1.html (17/05/01).

Pecotic, D. (2001), "Three Aboriginal Responses to New Age Religion. A Textual Interpretation", *Australian Religion Studies Review*, 14 (1).

Possamai-Inesedy, A. (2002), "Beck's Risk Society and Giddens' Search for Ontological Security: A Comparative Analysis between the Anthroposophical Society and the Assemblies of God", *Australian Religion Studies Review*, 15 (1): 27-43.

Possamai, A. (1999a), "The Aquarian Utopia of New Age", *Beyond the Divide*, (3): 68-79.

Possamai, A. (1999b), "Diversity in Alternative Spiritualities: Keeping New Age at Bay", *Australian Religion Studies Review*, 12 (2): 111-124.

Possamai, A. (2000a), "A Profile of New Agers: Social and Spiritual Aspects", *Journal of Sociology*, 36 (3): 345-358.

Possamai, A. (2000b), "A New Look at the Cultic Milieu", in Oakley *et al.* (eds.), *Sociological Sites/Sights*, TASA 2000 Conference Proceedings, Adelaide, CD-Rom.

Possamai, A. (2001a), "A Revisionist Perspective on Secularisation: Alternative Spiritualities, Globalised Consumer Culture, and Public Spheres", in C. Cusack and P. Oldmeadow (eds.), *The End of Religions? Religion in an Age of Globalization*, Sydney Studies in Religion (3): 200-215.

Possamai, A. (2001b), "Not the New Age: Perennism and Spiritual Knowledges", *Australian Religion Studies Review*, 14 (1): 82-96.

Possamai, A. (2003), "The Social Construction of Comic Books as a (Non) Recognised Form of Art in Australia", *Form/Work* 6: 109-121.

Possamai, A. (forthcoming) *In Search of New Age Spirituality*, UK, Ashgate.

Price, S. (2004), "Take a Pew at God's Café, Sit Back and Savour a Sermon", *The Sun Herald*, August 1: 23.

Redfield, J. (1994), *The Celestine Prophecy*, Sydney, Bantam.

Rendon, A. (2001), "Relearning from Las Vegas: Robert Venturi and the Politics of Postmodern Architecture", *Journal of Mundane Behaviour*, 2 (3): 291-307.

Reynolds, R. (1992), *Super Heroes: A Modern Mythology*, London, B.T. Batsford.

Richards, D. (1995), "Whitefella Dreaming", *HQ*, (May-June): 61-67.

Richardson, J. T. (1985), "Studies of Conversion: Secularization or Re-enchantment?" in Phillip E. Hammond (ed.), *The Sacred in a Secular Age. Toward Revision in the Scientific Study of Religion*, Berkeley and Los Angeles, California, University of California Press.

Riffard, P. A. (1990), *L'ésotérisme*, Paris, Robert Laffont.

Ritzer, G. (1999), *Enchanting a Disenchanted World: Revolutionizing the Means of Consumption*, California, Pine Forge Press.

Ritzer, G. (2000), *The Mcdonaldization of Society*, California, Pine Forge Press.

Roberts, R. (1994), "Power and Empowerment: New Age Managers and the Dialects of Modernity/Postmodernity", *Syzygy: Journal of Alternative Religion and Culture*, 3 (3-4): 271-288.

Robinson, W.G. (1997), "Heaven'sGate: The End?", *JCMC* 3 (3), Internet site, http://www.ascusc.org/jcmc/vol3/issue3/robinson.html (25/08/04).

Rojek, C. and B. Turner (eds.) (1993), *Forget Baudrillard?*, London, Routledge.

Roof, Wade Clark. (1999), *Spiritual Marketplace: Baby Boomers and the Remaking of American Religion*, Princeton, Princeton University Press.

Roof, Wade Clark, Jackson W. Carroll and David A. Roozen (eds.) (1995), *The Post-War Generation and Establishment Religion. Cross-Cultural Perspectives*, Boulder (USA) and London, Westview Press.

Romanowski, W. (2001), *Eyes Wide Open: Looking for God in Popular Culture*, Grand Rapids, Michigan, Brazos Press.

Rosenau, P. (1992), *Post-Modernism and the Social Sciences. Insight, Inroads, and Intrusions*, Princeton, New Jersey, Princeton University Press.

Ross, A. (1991), *Strange Weather. Culture, Science, and Technology in the Age of Limits*, New York.

Roszak, T. (1969), *The Making of a Counter Culture. Reflections on the Technocratic Society and its Youthful Opposition*, New York, Anchor Books.

Roszak, T. (1976), *Unfinished Animal. The Aquarian Frontier and the Evolution of Consciousness*, London, Faber And Faber.

Rothstein, M. (2003), "UFO Beliefs as Syncretic Components', in C. Partridge (ed.), *UFO Religions*, London, Routledge: 256-273.

Rushing, J. (1985), "E.T. as Rhetorical Transcendence", *Quarterly Journal of Speech*, 71 (2): 188-203.

Russell, B. (1960), *Religion and Science*, London, Oxford University Press.

Sabin, R. (1996), *Comics, Comix & Graphic Novels: A History of Comic Art*, New York, Phaidon Press.

Salisbury, M. (1999), *Writers on Comics Scriptwriting*, London, Titan books.

Savage, William Jr. (1990), *Commies, Cowboys, and Jungle Queens: Comic Books and America, 1945-1954*, Hanover and London, Wesletan University Press.

Savramis, D. (1987), "Religion et bandes dessinées: Tarzan et Superman sauveurs", *Social Compass*, 33 (1): 77-86.

Schechter, H. (1979), "Focus on Myth and American Popular Art", *Journal of American Culture*, 2 (2): 210-216.

Schick, C., J. Jaffe & A. Watkinson eds. (2004), *Contesting Fundamentalisms*, Halifax, Nova Scotia, Fernwood Publishing.

Schiller, H. (1996), *Information Inequality: The Deepening Social Crisis in America*, New York, Routledge.

Schlegel, J-L. (1995), *Religions à la carte*, Paris, Hachette.

Schnoebelen, W. (2001), "Should a Christian Play Dungeons & Dragons', Chick Publication, Internet site, http://www.chick.com.articles/frpg.asp (25/10/2002).

Schopp, A. (1997), "Cruising the Alternatives: Homoeroticism and the Contemporary Vampire", *Journal of Popular Culture*, 30: 231-243.

Screech, M. (1999), "André Franquin, Master of the Ninth Art", *Journal of Popular Culture*, 33 (3): 95-133.

Seay, C. and G. Garrett (2003), *The Gospel Reloaded: Exploring Spirituality and Faith in the Matrix*, Colorado Spring, Pinon Press.

Simmel, G. (1991), *Secret et sociétés secrètes*, Strasbourg, Circé.

Simmel, G. (1997), *Simmel on Culture*, D. Frisby and M. Featherstone (eds.), London, Sage.

Smith, H. (1989), *Beyond the Post-Modern Mind*, Wheaton, The Theosophical Publishing House.

Smith, B. (1994), "Modernism and Post-Modernism: Neo-Colonial Viewpoint", *Thesis 11*, (38): 104-117.

Smith, M. (1999), "Strands in the Web: Community-Building Strategies in Online Fanzines", *Journal of Popular Culture*, 33 (2): 87-99.

Stark, R. and W.S. Bainbridge (1985), *The Future of Religion. Secularization, Revival and Cult Formation*, Berkeley, University Of California Press.

Stark, R. and Laurence R. Iannaccone (1994), "A Supply-Side Reinterpretation of the "Secularization" of Europe", *Journal for the Scientific Study of Religion*, 33 (3): 230-252.

Stone, D. (1978), "New Religious Consciousness and Personal Religious Experience", *Sociological Analysis*, 39 (2): 123-134.

Street, J. (1997), *Politics and Popular Culture*, Cambridge, Polity Press.

Tacey, D. (2000), *Re-Enchantment. The New Australian Spirituality*, Sydney, Harper Collins.

Tamney, J. (2002), *The Resilience of Conservative Religion: The Case of Popular Conservative Protestant Congregations*, Cambridge, Cambridge University Press.

Taylor, B. (1997), "Earthen Spirituality or Cultural Genocide?: Radical Environmentalism's Appropriation of Native American Spirituality", *Religion*, 27: 183-215.

Trevelyan, G. (1984), *A Vision of the Aquarian Age. The Emerging Spiritual WorldView*, Walpole, New Hampshire, Stillpoint Publishing.

Troeltsch, E. (1950), *The Social Teaching of the Christian Churches*, two volumes, London, George Allen & Unwin.

Trueheart, C. (1996), "Welcome to the Next Church", *The Atlantic Monthly*, August: 37-58.

Truzzi, M. (1972), "The Occult Revival as Popular Culture: Some Random Observations on the Old and Nouveau Witch", *Sociological Quarterly*, (13): 16-36.

Tugend, T. (2001), "Arabs Step up War on Pokemon", *The Jerusalem Post*, April 29. Internet site, http://www.cesnur.org/2001/pokemon_april01.htm (27/02/04).

Van Hove, H. (1999), "L'émergence d'un 'marché spirituel' religieux", *Social Compass*, 46 (2): 161-172.

Volker, D. (1997), "De l'usage possible du concept troeltschien de religion dans les sciences sociales", *Revue de l'histoire des religions*, 214: 2

Walker, J. (1983), *Art in the Age of Mass Media*, London, Pluto Press.

Warner, S. R. (1993), "Work in Progress Toward a New Paradigm for the Sociological Study of Religion in the United States", *American Journal of Sociology*, 98 (5): 1044-93.

Weber, M. (1968), *The Protestant Ethic and the Spirit of Capitalism*, London, Unwin University Books.

Weber, M. (1970), *From Max Weber: Essays in Sociology*, translated, edited and with an introduction by H.H. Gerth and C. Wright Mills, London, Routlegde & Kegan Paul.

Wedgwood, C. (1930), "The Nature and Functions of Secret Societies", *Oceania*, 1 (2): 129-145.

Welch, C. (2002), "Appropriating the Didjeridu and the Sweat Lodge: New Age Baddies and Indigenous Victims?", *Journal of Contemporary Religion*, 17 (1): 21-38.

Werbner, P. (1995), "Powerful Knowledge in a Global Sufi Cult: Reflections on the Poetics of Travelling Theories", in *The Pursuit of Certainty: Religious and Cultural Formulations*, W. James (ed.), London, Routledge: 134-160.

Wertham, F. (1996), "The Psychopathology of Comic Books: A Symposium", *American Journal of Psychotherapy*, 50 (4): 417-436.

Westley, F. (1978), "'The Cult of Man': Dukheim's Predictions and New Religious Movements", *Sociological Analysis*, 39 (2): 135-145.

Williams, Dale E. (1984), *"2001: A Space Odyssey*: A Warning Before Its Time", *Critical Studies in Mass Communication*, 1, 311-321.

Williams, H. (2003), "Two Can Play That Game: Hollywood and the Games Industry Are Getting Closer Than Ever", *The Guardian Weekly*, January, 16-22: 22.

Winslade, J. (2000), "Techno-Kabbalah: The Performative Language of Magick and the Production of Occult Knowledge", *The Drama Review*, 44 (2): 84-100.

Wuthnow, R. (2001), "Spirituality and Spiritual Practice', in *The Blackwell Companion to Sociology of Religion*, R. Fenn (ed.), Oxford, Blackwell: 306-320.

York, M. (1995), *The Emerging Network. A Sociology of the New Age and Neo-Pagan Movements*, Maryland, Rowmann & Littlefield Publishers.

York, M. (1999), "Le supermarché religieux: ancrages locaux du Nouvel Age au sein du réseau mondial", *Social Compass*, 46 (2): 173-179.

York, M. (2001a), "Selling Nature in the Spiritual Supermarket", Cesnur Center for Studies on New Religions. Internet site, http://www.cesnur.org/2001/london2001/york.htm (30/04/01).

York, M. (2001b), "New Age Commodification and Appropriation of Spirituality", *Journal of Contemporary Religion*, 16 (3): 361- 372.

Zaidman, N. (2003), "Commercialization of Religious Objects: A Comparison Between Traditional and New Age Religions", *Social Compass*, 50 (3): 345-360.

"Gods, Humans and Religions"

While most traditional world religions seem to face a fundamental identity and cultural crisis, signs are indicating that there is a universal need for new spiritual demands and revival, new awakenings of religious practices and feelings. What are the facts beyond these movements? Is there a new human religiosity in the making?

This series brings together witnesses, thinkers, believers and non-believers, historians, scientists of religion, theologians, psychologists, sociologists, philosophers and general writers, from different cultures and languages, to offer a broader perspective on one of the key issues of our new world civilization in the making.

Series Editor: Gabriel FRAGNIÈRE,
Former Rector of the College of Europe (Bruges),
Président du Forum Europe des Cultures

Published Books

No.10– Christiane TIMMERMAN & Walter NONNEMAN, Dirk HUTSEBAUT, Walter VAN HERCK & Sara MELS (eds.), *Faith-based Radicalism Christianity, Islam and Judaism between Constructive Activism and Destructive Fanaticism*, 2007, ISBN 978-90-5201-050-2

No.9– Pauline CÔTÉ & T. Jeremy GUNN (eds.), *La nouvelle question religieuse. Régulation ou ingérence de l'État ? / The New Religious Question. State Regulation or State Interference?*, 2006, ISBN 978-90-5201-034-2

No.8– Wilhelm DUPRÉ, *Experience and Religion. Configurations and Perspectives*, 2005, ISBN 978-90-5201-279-7

No.7– Adam POSSAMAI, *Religion and Popular Culture. A Hyper-Real Testament*, 2005 (2nd printing 2007), ISBN 978-90-5201-272-8

N° 6– Gabriel FRAGNIÈRE, *La religion et le pouvoir. La chrétienté, l'Occident et la démocratie*, 2005 (2nd printing 2006), ISBN 978-90-5201-268-1

No.5– Christiane TIMMERMAN & Barbara SEGAERT (eds.), *How to Conquer the Barriers to Intercultural Dialogue. Christianity, Islam and Judaism*, 2005 (2nd printing 2006), ISBN 978-90-5201-258-2

N° 4– Elizabeth CHALIER-VISUVALINGAM, *Bhairava: terreur et protection. Mythes, rites et fêtes à Bénarès et à Katmandou*, 2003, ISBN 978-90-5201-173-8

No.3– John Bosco EKANEM, *Clashing Cultures. Annang Not(with)standing Christianity – An Ethnography*, 2002, ISBN 978-90-5201-983-3

No.2– Peter Chidi OKUMA, *Towards an African Theology. The Igbo Context in Nigeria*, 2002, ISBN 978-90-5201-975-8

No.1– Karel DOBBELAERE, *Secularization: An Analysis at Three Levels*, 2002 (2nd printing 2004), ISBN 978-90-5201-985-7